KISS
FEWER
FROGS

D0786155

KISS FEWER FROGS

The Fast Track Secret to Your Fairy Tale Ending

JAMES SHERIDAN

AUTHOR OF *THE YOU CODE*

DUDLEY COURT PRESS
SONOITA, AZ

"It's kind of fun to do the impossible."

—WALT DISNEY

Contents

part one

ALL
WISHED
UP

"Someday" Is Not a Strategy

"Once upon a time, there was a princess . . ."

With saucer eyes, my four-year-old daughter, Scarlett, hung on my every word as I read her favorite bedtime story for the third time that week. We both loved the "happily ever after" ending, but only one of us was buying how the princess got there.

Scarlett's mother caught the familiar brick-throwing look on my face, rolled her eyes, and left the room. But I resisted the temptation of doing an on-the-spot rewrite or hurling the storybook across the room and telling my daughter how it *really* happens. A big part of being a parent involves protecting my little girl from harsh truths such as, "Yeah, but some princes are just out to get laid and never call you again, so here's how to spot *those* clowns a mile away!" Most of all, I couldn't blow her tiny mind with what would soon be called "groundbreaking" and award-winning research that I was knee-deep into *if* I said, "But, princess, here's the good news: *there are only seven different types of princes to choose from.* Know these different types, and the mystery about men will vanish. You will see that there is no one-size-fits-all dating advice. You'll also see that there is no Prince Perfect, but there *is* a prince who's perfect for *you.* And, with this power, you will be able to capture that man's heart in a way that not even his own mother could. You will know him better than he knows himself. As a result, you will possess the key to his *soul.*"

My daughter has many years ahead to slowly absorb the impact of all my bombshells, but *you* don't. Your time is now, so put on your hard hat.

There is no rainbow without first experiencing rain. If you're reading this book, you are living proof that every other dating/relationship strategy you've studied to this point (and I bet a dollar to a donut you've tried them all) misses the mark to some degree, or you'd be happily married by now, right?

But it's not your fault, because you've been trying to hit a target while wearing a blindfold. Those smug married friends of yours? They just happened to bump into someone while blindfolded, God love them, so it's pure luck if they *truly* did find The One (cue Happy-Life brochure that exists only on their Facebook page).

Usually, people just settle and suffer. But don't resign yourself to such a last-resort fate. You can and *will* have your "fairy tale ending" if you're open-minded enough to let me rewrite the script, *and* for me to teach you how to fast track it, it so it happens shockingly quicker. Then you will kiss *far* fewer frogs along the way.

Most men need love just as much as women. The key difference is that, as contradictory as it may seem, most single men aren't *consciously* going around looking for love. Sex? Always. But love? In guys' locker rooms, you'll hear bedpost-notch pissing contests, harrowing accounts from "marriage-prison-camp" survivors, and overdramatized stalker stories. But the guy who says aloud, "That's great, y'all, but I'm looking for *lurve* . . ." will attract strange looks, ridicule, and a towel-slap across his "sissy-ass" face. If he's more fortunate (perhaps it happens at the golf club instead of the gym), the other guys will quietly treat him as if he's mentally handicapped from that day forward. (By the way, if you're thinking about fact-checking anything I tell you in this book with your male friends or relatives, don't expect an honest answer, lest they violate Guy Code. "Oh, this Sheridan guy's got that all wrong. *I'm* not like that," they'll say, looking at the floor. What, you think we'd admit to *you* how we really can be?)

So, our mission (yes, I'm coming with you) is to find that poor, towel-slapped guy—even if he was dumb enough to state his noble intentions aloud—*and*, most importantly, making sure he's the specific brand of husband material that's right for *you*. Kissing fewer frogs means applying an ultrathick filter so you don't waste time with a man who 1) isn't serious about finding a life partner at this time or 2) is an incompatible life partner for you. Point 2 is the real game-changer here.

You know that moment, perhaps several months into a relationship, when a single event or something he does or says makes you end it suddenly? Well, assuming you're not psychotically OCD and the event isn't just him brushing his teeth clockwise instead of anti-clockwise, those often long-awaited surprises are over. You can see into the future with what you'll learn in this book.

Yes, you can stop wasting valuable time determining if a man is suitable for you through *years* of trial and error or being strung along by commitment-phobes. You've probably been told it takes at least two years to see if a partner is suited for life (and the players who would merrily waste two years of your life *love* this conventional "wisdom"). But I'm going to show you how to know if a man is the right husband material for you or not *within ten minutes of your first contact*. This won't sound insane by the end of Part Two and Part Six, trust me.

Chemistry is the one thing you can't control and that I can't predict. As you well know, that magic simply happens or it doesn't. But chemistry can fade, and it isn't enough by itself to reveal if that particular man is a suitable life partner for you.

Conventional wisdom says there's no way we can know how a relationship will be until we're actually in the middle of it. I say that's wrong. Sure, some things you can't know for certain, such as which side of the bed he'll sleep on or cataclysmic unforeseen events like a disabling car crash. But you *can* know how accommodating he'd be about switching sides of the bed or what he might do in the event of a disabling car crash. You *can* know what drives him, what makes him behave the way he does, what makes this *particular* man happy or sad, how romantic he's inclined to be, how reliable he's likely to be, how career-focused he's leaning toward being, and so on.

The point is you will experience no surprises later in life once you've made your selection. You won't have to waste precious years building a psychological profile on potential suitors. Heck, when it comes to weeding out the deal-breakers, you won't even need to kiss the guy.

Once you've made your choice from the Seven Princes you'll meet, you will know all you need to know about him, what's really important to know, and something even he doesn't know: who he really is and what his purpose is in life. *You will understand him.* And this makes you his queen, his priestess, the woman he will cherish and elevate above all other women, his *equal team partner.* No amount of "pretty" holds a candle to this kind of oneness.

When you're walking through life blindfolded, wishing and waiting is all you have. But the knowledge in this book gives you the power that removes the blindfold, and I'm not talking about some generalized and tired fatherly wisdom—that is, sitting you on my knee while I get out the Werther's Original caramels. I'm talking about precise, game-changing steps that will dramatically change the course of your life—forever. All you have to do is follow these steps.

Being surgically precise and calculatingly proactive in dating has never been more possible because, now, you'll have a clear idea about what exactly you're looking for. And you'll know how to quickly filter out what you're *not* looking for, *based on the reality of what's on offer.* You and I can work with a *defined, authentic goal to shoot for* instead of the usual circle-talk shit-show that most people pass off as a dating strategy.

For both men and women, romantic relationships are the foundations of a fulfilled life, so why should you go about getting one in such a haphazard fashion?

Having a decent job is a life goal to take seriously and act accordingly. Why not act the same way when it comes to relationships? If you want a job, do you dance around in your pajamas singing, "Someday my Fortune-500-employer-with-benefits will come . . . "? No, you get busy. You exaggerate your resume, return your sweatpants to the lost-the-will-to-live drawer, shovel on the makeup, and devise a plan to actively target certain employers. Then you sign up to recruitment agencies. Listen . . .

♛

If you want something in life, there can be no half
measures. You either go all in with verve or step off
and be happy as you are. But don't sit on the fence
and complain.

I have a hunch that the saying "good things come to those who
wait" was invented by commitment-phobes and players who happily
waste precious years of your life while you make excuses for them,
and while your "friends" assure you he will change. Fear of both
being alone and of the unknown keeps you prisoner and playing it
safe—until the relationship ends. And with that ending go years of
your life. Know this:

♛

Your fear will take you to
whatever it is you're afraid of.

When it comes to meeting guys, this probably isn't your first rodeo
(and if it is, well done for buying this book; you just saved yourself
a divorce or two). And, after falling so many times, it's hard to get
back in the game. But know this: you're not getting back into that
game; you're about to play a very different game in which you have
a grossly unfair advantage over the other players, both male and
female.

"Someday" your prince may well come, just as "someday" you may
win the lottery. But "someday" is not a strategy. To kiss fewer frogs, you
need to take control of what's on offer. By waiting and wishing for

your prince to come, you've positioned yourself as a helpless female. You put yourself beneath a much more capable male who does the choosing, instead of being *equals*, a *team*, a foundation of *unconditional love* needed for a lasting and deeply happy relationship. That all changes, here and now. *"Once upon a time there was a princess . . ."* is as far as *your* story goes before your big rewrite.

Broaden Your Horizon

> *"It ain't what you don't know that gets you into trouble.*
> *It's what you know for sure that just ain't so."*
>
> — MARK TWAIN

For me to fill your cup with new knowledge, you must first empty that cup. Or, in those guttural words of Yoda, "You must unlearn what you have learned." So, let's begin.

Weeks from now, when you're snuggled up on the couch with popcorn, watching this blockbuster romantic movie with your new boyfriend, you'll have this fun fact to tell him, only adding to his wonder of you . . .

On April 10, 1912, the British luxury passenger liner *Titanic* set sail on her maiden voyage. Four days later, the ship hit an iceberg and sank, leaving many questions unanswered about why and how it could have happened. But there is one question that begs to be answered the most: why did two of the most experienced lookout crew members in the White Star Line fail to see the iceberg until it was too late?

Many factors contributed to the sinking, including the ship's inappropriately high speed. But, in the final analysis, had the lookouts seen the iceberg sooner, *Titanic* would likely have avoided hitting it. She nearly *did* miss the iceberg; it was precisely because she merely grazed it that the edge of the iceberg sliced through five of its hull compartments like a knife.

Bear with me, I promise you this is going somewhere relevant . . .

Recent research shows the most convincing theory to date about why the *Titanic* catastrophe happened. Multiple accounts from eyewitnesses in *Titanic*'s lifeboats corroborate the meteorological phenomenon that was in play that night (that were well-depicted in the movie): before the iceberg hit the hull, the weather was suddenly and unusually clear and cold, with many stars in view in the night sky, *and the smoke from Titanic's stacks dramatically changed direction fifty to a hundred feet above.* An unusually cold and fast-moving air mass from the Arctic had descended on the vessel, causing a "cold water mirage." When driving, you know how heat on the road ahead can make it seem as though the horizon is lower than it actually is? The reverse can happen with cold air, making it appear as though the horizon is *higher* than it is. *Titanic*'s lookouts had a false perception of where the horizon was; they were looking higher than the actual horizon. In the darkness, that iceberg slipped under their scan until it was too late.

Similarly, too many people are on a collision course with disaster because they're simply not looking in the right place, due to a faulty worldview. It's time to shift your perspective to ensure you are dealing with *reality*, not illusion. Only then can you reach your goal.

When your worldview is accurate,
not artificial—like the view *Titanic's* lookouts had
—you'll stop courting disaster.

By the way, do you recall one of the hidden magic ingredients of the movie *Titanic's* huge success, especially with women? Jack didn't come to Rose's rescue as much as she came to his. They were equals behaving as a team. Rose didn't wish and wait; she transformed into a badass and made it happen.

Acknowledging two Big Lies and two Big Revelations will ensure we don't have an artificial worldview. Let's begin with the lies . . .

BIG LIE #1: Prince Perfect

There is no such thing as a perfect man. "Well, duh. Dude, fairy tales are just stuff we read to make our kids go to sleep. We don't take them seriously." Well, you may not *consciously* think that stories influence your beliefs, but Plato wasn't being a drama queen when he said, "Storytellers are dangerous people." The storytellers' power comes from influencing people unconsciously—with ideas slipping past the sentries of your conscious mind. It's a form of hypnotism. To an unprotected *child's* mind, in the formative years (under ten years old), these ideas become deeply rooted in an abstract way that affects behaviors and beliefs. In adulthood, ideas from childhood still influence your mentality without you realizing it—unless you become mindful of them, unless you become *conscious*.

Little boys aren't typically exposed to fairy tales; they only suffer them out the corner of their eye because their sister likes them and their mother dragged them along to the movie theater (although they do enjoy the part when the prince has to do battle with some kind of monster). So, in adulthood, men have no clue about the big act they have to follow: Prince Perfect.

If I haven't made this point clear already, I will do much more as the book goes on: *the average male is about as far from Prince Perfect as you can imagine.* This is a good fact to know, because when you see with your own eyes in this book how imperfect *every* man is, then you will feel less intimidated when you meet one who makes you swoon. You'll feel more worthy of him.

Young women typically start off with a checklist of requirements that their ideal husband must have. However, as they age and life delivers them a few punches, that checklist gets steadily eroded until they're just grateful for a guy who has his original teeth. But the basic idea of Prince Perfect still has an insidious grip on most women. This is true especially if you were overloved as a child. That means you were effectively told that no man would be good enough for you, and you were shown that love should be given to you without needing to reciprocate.

As females grow up, their young minds unconsciously regard how their fathers treated them as models for how future men *should* treat them. But "Daddy issues" can be problematic, not only if the father was neglectful, but also if he was overattentive and insisted that no man would ever be good enough for his little princess.

Of course, the opposite can also be true. That's when you needlessly suffer bad relationships because your father *under*loved you. By the way, experienced players and predators are aware of "Daddy issues," and the most cunning ones home in on women they perceive as having them, seeing them as easy targets. This won't be the last time we touch on "Daddy issues," but let's stay on the subject of Prince Perfect.

Also unconsciously influencing you are the media. We live in a world where you are surrounded by images of airbrushed perfection, online and offline, and this exposure can affect your idea of what men should look like and how they should act, depending on how much time you spend engrossed in media rather than real life. To the human brain, perception is reality. And the human brain is a comparing engine, so when it compares what it *perceives* as reality to actual reality, the conflict between the two can lead to unrealistic expectations. I suggest limiting your exposure to media and that you appreciate that only what you see in real life is real. Besides, you already know about things like makeup and special photo effects because you've likely tried online dating.

Fussiness and OCD issues on your part can also be a problem. If you think Prince Perfect should always wear black shirts for date nights and leave his slippers an inch apart at a ninety-degree angle to the bedside (you may laugh, but OCD people are cringing as they read this), then you will efficiently emasculate a man and/or make him get in his car and drive away—to anywhere, really fast.

I get it, because I can be a little OCD myself. But whenever I feel myself losing grip, I watch the movie *The Aviator* and tell myself not to be such a weirdo. That path only leads to peeing in bottles and never leaving the house or cutting your fingernails. Most important, this book is called *Kiss Fewer Frogs*, not *You'll Never Kiss Anyone EVER Again Because Nobody Could Possibly Navigate Your Minefield of Bullshit.*

There's a great moment in *The Aviator* when germophobe Howard Hughes likes a woman enough to actually let her drink from the same bottle as him, where he appreciates that love is far more important than the issues that make him so dysfunctional. Find that moment within yourself. In the not-too-distant future, you truly will be able to buy a robot husband you can program to your exact specifications, but until then, you'll have to work with humans.

The biggest point needed to smash the idea of Prince Perfect is this: you'll soon see that, as in all areas of life, a tradeoff will be involved when you choose your prince. All of the Seven Princes you'll meet have strengths and weaknesses by their *inherent nature*. It's not simply that they each have weaknesses; it's that they each have an ingrained and interrelated set of traits that stem from what's called a Dominant Driver, and you will need to make some sacrifices and prioritize. For example, wanting a guy who is driven by logic (mister safe-and-steady) to also be driven by creativity (mister passion-and-spontaneity) is, you'll soon see, totally unrealistic from the viewpoint of what comes *naturally* to each man. His traits don't come a la carte. You get a set menu and no substitutions (more about this soon). But know that *all* Seven Princes will sometimes be a pain in the ass, each in his own special way. Part of the choosing is figuring out which *kind* of ass-pain you can tolerate when balanced against which kind of *joy* that each prince is likely to bring you—forever and ever.

Finally, are *you* perfect? If you're saying yes right now, then refer back to Daddy issues of the overloved variety. For everyone else, the answer is no. Then, why should you expect your life partner to be perfect if you aren't?

Nothing said here precludes having standards of how you expect to be treated—*au contraire*, as Part Four will hammer home. But what I am saying here is that you *should* have a vivid picture of the man you're looking for. But the pictures have already been drawn for you, none of them are perfect, and you simply need to pick one.

BIG LIE #2: "I will change him/he will change"

The relationship graveyard is littered with tombstones that have this lie chiseled onto them, and well-intentioned (?) friends of the deceased have often dug the holes. *R.I.P. John and Jane. "He said he would change."* Afflicted relationships that didn't die from this lie became zombie-like instead.

The second Big Lie is a legacy of the first Big Lie. The Prince Perfect lie is so deep-rooted in the mind that, once a woman sees firsthand her chosen man has a flaw, she convinces herself that part of his personality can be surgically removed—often by her. Be aware:

People believe what they want to believe.
That is true for you too.

When you have a vested interest in an outcome, you're inclined to develop a thesis about that outcome being favorable, so you tend to then only acknowledge information that fits your thesis and to ignore information that contradicts it. This phenomenon is called confirmation bias, and the relationship graveyard isn't the only cemetery that it sponsors. Many *real* graves result from it, too.

"But people *can* and *do* change!" I hear you and Hollywood cry. You both make a good point, so let's next clarify what I mean when I declare that he won't change. Here are opening excerpts from my award-winning book, *The You Code*:

> *There is an old saying: Leopards can't change their spots. In other words, it's in our nature to act a certain way and our basic personality never changes . . . Each leopard will have a different nurture experience since birth, but they are still leopards . . . Humans are inclined to polarize opinions, so we take extreme sides on the "nature versus nurture" argument, but the reality is that both our nature and our nurture unconsciously affect our behavior. With awareness and perhaps professional help we can identify and overcome the nurtured behaviors that can be so self-sabotaging, and this is the side of us that we can and should change. But trying to change the nature we're born with is like trying to separate our shadow; it's who we are.*

So, yes, you can pressure him to stop smoking or drinking. You can urge him to get professional help and deal with childhood issues (and, who knows, the money might even be well spent), *but he is the man he was born as.* You know this from experience; it's just that when you're emotionally involved, you ignore the benefit of that experience. For example, whenever you have an intervention with others about their behavior, professionally or personally, have you noticed they only briefly change their ways before returning to their *natural state*, their baseline performance level? It's like pushing or pulling on a rubber band; eventually it pings back. The Universe has an uncanny way of making things revert to the mean, and to fight this truth is to fight the laws of nature. But salvation awaits for those who don't fight nature and instead harness its power . . .

♛

Go with the flow;
just make sure you choose
the right river to flow with.

Each of the Seven Princes has his own kind of nature, and you will soon become aware of each so you can choose an appropriate "river" to flow with. Speaking of rivers, do you remember hearing this story when you were young?

> *A scorpion asked a frog a question: "I want to get across the river. If I sit on your back, will you swim me across?" The frog replied, "No! If I do that, you'll sting me to death." The scorpion said, "Why would I do that? If I did, you'd sink, and we would both drown." The frog accepted the scorpion's explanation and agreed to the request. Halfway across the river, the scorpion stung the frog. Sinking, the frog said, "Why did you do that? Now we will both die!" The scorpion said, "I'm sorry. It's just my nature." Both the scorpion and the frog drowned.*

As a child being told that story, I wasn't upset with the scorpion for being a scorpion. I merely thought, "That frog was a dumbass." (I had a potty mouth even as a kid.) "I mean, what kind of a moron would do that?" Son, adults do it to themselves all the time. Maybe the frog had a thing for the scorpion.

Soon you will know to stop trying to change a man's immovable nature. Instead, you'll decisively move on to a different man whose nature *is* more to your liking. Don't worry, I'll soon show you how to spot "scorpions" a mile away, and awareness of Big Lie #2 will help you reach your HOOYA! moment. The H.O.O.Y.A.! moment happens when you see clearly and shout, "Hooya!" because you finally took your **H**ead **O**ut **O**f **Y**our **A**ss.

Consider Hooya! to be the antidote to the poison of confirmation bias. But far too often, the antidote comes too late, so please know:

♛

Rewards go to the realist.

This won't be the last time you'll read that line in this book. I've coached thousands of women across the globe over the past two decades, especially one-on-one relationship coaching after *The You Code* was released. Coaching them to be realists was both the hardest and most rewarding part of the process for both of us. Most of these women were emotionally adrift in desperately unhappy marriages. Everything turned a corner after they accepted that their husband's nature wasn't changing. These women either needed to learn to love their spouse or choose another animal.

Assuming the relationship wasn't straight-up abusive but more about differences, I found it helped to ask, "Don't you want your husband to love you *just the way you are*? Yes? Then, doesn't he deserve the same?"

Luckily, you get to choose well from the beginning. I will help you to do so extremely quickly—*before emotions can cloud your judgment and confirmation bias takes hold!* But, if you're a control freak who is still hell-bent on changing people, hang tight. I have something special coming up, and I don't mean Xanax.

Next, let's take a more constructive turn by discussing the two Big Revelations. After all, to get different results, you have to do something different.

Let me present you with new ideas to challenge your long-held beliefs and perhaps frighten your ego. If you're proceeding with skepticism, bitterness, or a know-it-all attitude (all three attributes the product of fear), you can expect failure, thereby making yourself right but still alone. Failure is the easiest goal to accomplish, which is why it's such a popular goal. Open your mind to a new approach.

BIG REVELATION #1: There is no such thing as "men"

This game-changing revelation can dramatically change your relationship with men, because it changes how you *view* men. When you say, "men are this" or "men are that"—especially if preceded by the word "all"—you're generalizing. This thinking isn't only lazy and prejudicial; you simply can't kiss fewer frogs if you believe all frogs are alike.

The seven types of men are *shockingly* different from one another (not precluding the basic commonalities we'll talk about in Part Four). I'm sure you appreciate we've all had different upbringings, which makes us different. But the difference between these seven male types I'll show you is their *nature*; it's how they were born.

(This follows from Big Lie #2 explaining you can't change a person's basic nature.) This also means that, when it comes to what *really* makes a guy who he is, you have only seven types to choose from *and* it's nonsensical to generalize. Once you see how different each of the seven profiles is, you'll appreciate this knowledge.

So, I'm not talking about random *nurtured* differences between these seven male types. Rather, I'm talking about *hardwired* tendencies, their *nature*, as I offer these examples:

"Men just aren't romantic." *Some* men aren't.

"Men can't express emotions, especially about love." *Some* men can't, and some men can't *help* but express their emotions!

"Men are all too career focused." *Some* men are.

"Men are such terrible listeners." *Some* men are.

"Men expect women to do housework and look after kids." *Some* men expect that.

"Men are all cheaters." *Some* men have a higher tendency than others toward infidelity.

"If a man likes me, he'll come over and introduce himself." *Some* men will. That last example has *huge* implications for dating (more on that later).

Let me share actual questions from women I've coached, followed by my replies that enabled them to either quickly move on to a more suitable choice *or* understand that man better, to know him better than he knows himself, and attain a deep bond with him:

"By continually showing up late, is this guy not interested in me?" *If he's Type 5, that's just his nature, not to excuse his lateness, but it doesn't mean he doesn't like you.*

"This guy refuses to tell me he loves me, so he can't be that into me." *Or he could just be Type 1.*

"This guy seems to like me one minute but not the next. Which is it?" *Relax, he's just a Type 3, and if he didn't like you, he certainly wouldn't be with you.*

"This guy loves being around women; he must be a player." *Or a Type 4.*

"This guy never wants to leave his house with me. Is he ashamed to take me out?" *Probably not if he's a Type 2.*

"He always says how much he needs his space, so he just can't like me, right?" *Wrong, and definitely a Type 2!*

"I can't seem to have a deep conversation with this guy. Is he holding back?" *No, he's a Type 6.*

"I read a dating book that said if a guy likes me, he'll *always* approach me." *Then the guy who wrote that book was a Type 7.*

"This guy will never admit he's wrong." *Well, Type 7s generally won't.*

Because I was answering problems in those examples, my replies highlighted inherent flaws in each type, but don't forget that each type also comes with different *but related* inherent benefits. Also, appreciate how each example references that man's *nature*, like the scorpion's, meaning he isn't going to change. As noted in *The You Code*:

This is powerful in the peace it brings you because personal
suffering partially ends when you stop arguing with other
people's unchangeable nature, you stop giving piggyback
rides to scorpions, and you instead celebrate our invisible
diversity.

Did you hear me? *He isn't going to change*—not at your hand, not
at his mother's hand, and not at God's hand (especially when God
is the one responsible).

♛

And why should he change?
Do you plan to change the nature
you were born with?

I hope not, and if so, I wish you luck.

So, instead of fighting this reality, *use it* to remove the mystery
about *types* of men—and to make a deep connection with your
chosen man—by appreciating there is no such thing as "men."

If your relationship history seems like one long Groundhog Day
because you "always seem to attract a certain kind of guy," now you
perhaps know why: because you're only drawn to *or selected by*
one of seven in a clone army. As people, we aren't as "special" as our
egos would have us believe. What makes us each feel "special" is the
smorgasbord of unique nurtures between us. But nurture is merely
scratches on the surface of the rock that is our inherent nature.

Yes, there really are plenty of fish in the sea, but only seven different
kinds of fish. And, better than the sea, these fish are all in conveniently marked barrels, and you're the only one shooting at

them unless every single woman buys this book (in my publisher's dreams!). Are you starting to realize that, other than the basics, using one-size-fits-all dating advice has limited use? Can you begin to see that "The One Who Got Away" has been cloned and you can find "him" again? Yes, provided there is chemistry, you can have "him" back, only this time do it right.

BIG REVELATION #2: You can *empower* him

This is the consolation prize if the Big Lie about not being able to change him disgruntled you. No, you can't change his nature, but you can *empower* him. This refers again to the power of knowing a man better than he knows himself, even better than his own mother knows him (more in Part Two).

Men and women have much more in common than you might think, including the basic human condition of searching for meaning; consciously or unconsciously asking the questions, "Who am I and why am I here?" Knowing the answers to these questions gives a person peace and clarity as they become conscious of their duality of nature and nurture. When a person knows truly who they are, the reason why they're here is only a logical step away. *Know Thyself* is the most succinct and powerful piece of advice ever given.

It stands to reason, then, that knowing the inherent nature of your chosen prince—the blueprint of his very spirit—enables you to *instantly* know him at a level of intimacy that will blow his mind. Doing this for a living—trust me—and watching people's jaws drop when they realize the power they have is addicting. But for the purpose of dating, this level of intimacy is too powerful for your subject to handle in one sitting. Even though you will have the knowledge, you don't want to slap him in the face with it at your first meeting.

People generally either don't trust who they think they are, or they simply don't see it. Either way, they are lost. But you can be their compass. I know this sounds crazy right now (I warned you before we began), but in Part Two, I'll explain further.

When you meet the Seven Princes, you'll also see the truth of these types for yourself as you quickly recognize male friends and relatives, and, yes, your exes. You'll slap your forehead and say, "So *that's* why that guy was such a _____!" What you write in that blank space could equally be a positive as a negative, as you'll soon see. Where there is darkness, there is light, and vice versa.

If change is a drag and empowerment is bliss—which of those two would you bestow upon a man? Choose well, and I can guarantee that he will never have met a woman like you. Now, *that's* a fairy-tale moment.

Can Dreams Come True?

You know that older couple, in their eighties, still in love as ever? They're holding hands and stroking each other; he's opening the door for her, and she's feeding him as they gaze into each other's bifocals. One day, that will be you and your life partner because that "special someone" truly is out there waiting to find you, too. You only have to find one person, and I hope you are starting to see how it's no longer like trying to find the proverbial needle in a haystack.

The travesty isn't the idea of a fairy tale ending itself. It's that most people don't have one because they don't know how to get one or what it entails. Your fairy tale ending is no longer an invisible and moving target when you know the "cheat codes," when you know how to fast track yours.

I'm not here to stomp all over your dreams; *I'm here to make them come true.* We will make your dreams come true by giving them *authentic definition* and a chronological sequence of steps to take to make the dreams reality. This means working smart instead of hard.

I believe in destiny, but I also believe we have a *responsibility to meet destiny.* Destiny is defined as "the events that will necessarily happen to a particular person in the future." This implies that, in order to believe in destiny, we must have a way to make predictions about what could happen to any given person in the future. Unless you believe in fortune-telling, predicting a person's behavior seems like a stretch of the imagination. Sure, we can't control many events in the future, and this is a comforting belief for many because it relinquishes us from any responsibility for our lives, but deep down we sense that we can, in fact, control some events.

We *do* have a large degree of control over our destiny because we constantly see the results of cause and effect as proof. For example, by deciding to write this book and stating it as my destiny to do so, with the subsequent act of tapping on the keys, my destiny came to pass, and lo and behold, I'm a fortune-teller! I wouldn't have been able to control a bus running me over before I typed the first word, but, barring the highly unlikely, I have *created* my destiny.

You *can* create your destiny up to a certain point too, depending on the storyline you choose. I'm about to present you with seven different fairy-tale storylines, seven different romantic destinies with seven different men, but it will be up to you to step up and meet them with your best foot forward.

With the Big Lies behind you and the Big Revelations guiding you, you can say farewell to the wishing well as you drive your dream forward. Hi-ho, let's go.

part two

CHOOSE A DISH OR GO HUNGRY

Hungry for Answers

You're about to meet your future husband. Behind the curtain are seven great guys waiting to meet you, each of them incredibly different, and each of them offering a different relationship experience. But before I pull back the curtain for you to make your selection, please carefully read the briefing notes that follow. They will help you choose wisely and appreciate the validity of these seven distinct types of males. Also, accept that you can't *change* the characteristics about any type you don't like.

On the subject of relationships, much has been said about the differences between men and women, but 1) you will soon see how these differences are not as far apart as you've been told, and 2) virtually *nothing* has been said about the differences in nature among *all* people, regardless of sex or gender. These disparities, I would argue, are at least as stark as the differences between men and women.

You've likely scratched your head about male behavior many times, but haven't you also scratched your head about the inherent and immoveable behavior of some of your girlfriends? You keep saying, "Different strokes for different folks." The good news is that there are only fourteen different strokes for fourteen different folks (seven male and seven female).

Choosing someone to spend the rest of your life with looms large, so I owe you a deeper explanation about these seven male types based on a cloned template of their very nature—the blueprint of their souls. You will see proof for yourself as you recognize every man you've ever known in the lineup. Have faith in the process. And if you've already read *The You Code*, feel free to move on to the next section, Decisions, Decisions.

Two explanations exist for having these seven types of males (females, too, but we address only males in this book). One is spiritual; one is scientific. Yet these two explanations can coexist.

The Spiritual Explanation

There are seven "soul blueprints" that become the consciousness and life force of a human body at conception. (Scientists cannot explain or locate consciousness in the human anatomy.) At death, a soul leaves the human body only to regenerate and enter a new body. It's the principle of eternal life, reincarnation, dreams, and déjà vu that are respected in ancient religions to this day. Indeed, as explained in *The You Code*, all religions essentially espouse the same concept—that our souls are eternal—but in their own ways.

Humankind began in East Africa 2.5 million years ago, so it makes sense that the ancient Egyptian religion is our closest link to our oldest beliefs. It's a religion epitomized by the *ankh*, a symbol of eternal life (and of male and female philosophies in perfect balance and harmony). Approximately 70,000 years ago, humans began leaving East Africa and migrated across the planet, carrying this ancient religion in their backpacks; hence, we see pyramids in

Mexico as well as Egypt. As spinoff factions of the Egyptian religion were founded around the world, a common spiritual belief in the regeneration of souls spread, too.

When friends and family congratulated me for *The You Code* winning an award and taking the #1 spot in Amazon's category for Evolutionary Psychology, their next question was, "What the hell is evolutionary psychology?" Evolutionary psychologists contend that contemporary human behavior, at least at an unconscious level, is often a legacy of our ancient past. That's a no-brainer when you think about it. If humans have been around for 2.5 million years, even the past ten thousand years represents only 0.4 percent of human existence. And what we call "modern day"—the past two hundred years—is only 0.008 percent of human existence!

Why only seven souls for each sex? Who knows? Maybe God got lazy and hoped we wouldn't notice (most of us still haven't!). *Or* maybe God had a set *purpose* for each of these different souls, which, *when working together*, would make a badass team (hence, Homo sapiens conquered all other human species), and this is where we dovetail with the scientific explanation . . .

The Scientific Explanation

Genetic changes don't happen overnight. Just because, in contemporary society with its perpetually shifting social narrative, humans decide that certain behaviors aren't desirable, that doesn't make them go away. Overcoming any primitive *unconscious* tendencies requires a *conscious effort*. Imagine driving your car at 70 miles an hour and suddenly another car appears right in front of you. You stomp on the brakes, but your car won't stop instantly due to momentum. Expecting that to happen is the same as expecting our lengthy ancient programming to not have any effect on us in modern life.

The You Code explains how these seven types of males and females could be a result of ancient tribal roles continually implanted as genetic memories that still influence us today. Each of these types is referred to as "Genetypes" (pronounced jen-na-types).

In 1916, long before I defined Genetypes, a psychoanalyst named Carl Jung offered this explanation (italics mine): "The collective unconscious comprises in itself the *psychic life of our ancestors* right back to the earliest beginnings. It is the matrix of all conscious psychic occurrences, and hence it *exerts an influence that compromises the freedom of consciousness* in the highest degree, since it is continually striving to lead all conscious processes back into the old paths . . . This collective unconscious does not develop individually but is *inherited*. It consists of *pre-existent* forms."

Sigmund Freud concurred with Jung's thesis in that he cited *archaic remnants*—mental images that could not be explained by anything in the subjects' lives—in their minds. Jung described the phenomenon as *"imprints or momentous or frequently recurring situations in the lengthy human past."*

From *The You Code:*

> *My Genetypal Theory builds on Jung's work with the benefit of genetic science and a decade-long endeavor to fully flesh out the Genetypes in a way that contemporary individuals can easily find themselves, their purpose, and*

hence, their new life map. Over the past six years, with thousands of people from a cross section of societies and backgrounds, I've conducted a multitude of trials and focus groups in different countries, testing and honing the theory, and the results have continually astounded me as much as the subjects. I would send the group to take an hour to study the Genetypal blueprints, and one hundred percent of the participants would return with a shocked expression on their often-tearful faces as they held up their Genetype profiles.

To circle back to Part One, *nurture* can be described as the scratches on the surface of the rock that is our *nature*—our Genetype. Nurture's artificial flavorings give us the *impression* that each of us is unique —and to a superficial extent, we *are* unique. But what matters most—what represents our immoveable nature, our spirit, our true and uncorrupted self—is our Genetype. And you'll find the Seven Princes are presented to you in Genetype form.

When Jack Canfield, co-author of *Chicken Soup for the Soul,* interviewed me about Genetypes, I referenced a story in his book that compared a person's Genetype (true self) to a golden statue covered in mud as a result of nurture. It's a good metaphor, for the ultimate goal of every human is to remove the mud (nurture, false self) and liberate the golden statue underneath (nature, true self)—that is, one's true spirit and purpose. You're about to see through the "mud" on any man.

Now, let me help you choose your prince.

Decisions, Decisions

As the saying goes, "The secret to a long marriage is to not get divorced." But that's only possible if you can survive banging your head against a brick wall for many years. *Forever* is a long time, so take this selection process slowly and don't move on in this book until you've made your choice.

Remember, there's no more playing "Pin the Tail on the Donkey." You're now choosing a life partner with your eyes wide open to the magic of Genetypes. So, no random page flicking to let fate decide, or asking your mother or friends to choose, or picking whomever you think society wants you to choose. It's about what *you* want and what *you* believe will work for you in a life partner.

Here is the simple formula for a successful choice:

Compatibility + Chemistry = Life Partner

Chemistry is out of our hands; there's either "something there" or not. It can happen instantly or gradually; it can be temporary or permanent; it's usually needed to kindle the fire of a new relationship. But that fire needs a continual supply of fuel to keep burning, and that's where *compatibility* comes in.

Because chemistry isn't something you can plan for, find out which of the Seven Princes are most *compatible* with you. Then, in the later parts of this book, you'll be guided to make a plan that exposes you to as many of your chosen type as possible and increase the odds of finding that *chemistry*.

Because Genetypes are representations
of a person's inherent and unchanging nature,
your choice of prince is a choice
based on compatibility.

Ancient elders knew this formula of compatibility and chemistry, which is where the principle of an arranged marriage comes from. It's my belief that ancient shamans knew about Genetypes, and they based their matchmaking decisions on this knowledge. The true art of the matchmaker has been forgotten, corrupted, or chastised, but ancient elders wisely knew that young lovers' decisions would be based purely on chemistry with no concern for long-term compatibility. Therefore, they kept youngsters effectively locked indoors until a line of suitors was selected for them primarily based on *compatibility*. From there, they'd let chemistry make the final choice. (I know, the pity you must now feel for my young daughter . . .)

Here are several pointers about making a wise choice for compatibility:

Don't use a long-term solution to fix a short-term problem.

Humans tend to assume that tomorrow will be just like today, but it rarely is. We struggle with the future because, for most of human existence, there wasn't one to consider; we were too busy surviving today to worry about tomorrow. For example, perhaps you are a single parent and want a life partner. Realizing that children grow up and leave the nest in the blink of an eye, don't choose a partner based primarily on them needing a father figure; those can be found in other ways. Instead, think about long-term compatibility for *you*. Maybe you need a partner who is financially independent right now. However, that status could change, so don't be tempted to choose a type who appears affluent but may not be rich in the future. As another example, let's say you're working through certain issues right now and need alone time. But only if needing days alone is a *consistent part of your nature* should you choose a guy who also needs days of alone time.

Remember, your goal is to find the guy who matches *who you truly are and have always been*. I had previously said don't let your mother choose for you, which I stand by. But, remember, those who know us best can tell us *who we really are*, so keep an open mind when they express their thoughts.

Assume you can have any of the seven Genetypes; don't sell yourself short.

Once you see the description of your desired prince, don't get in your own way by letting self-esteem issues creep in. You will see the flaws in each prince, so don't put The One on a pedestal. With the power you'll intrinsically own, you can have any prince you desire who is "on the menu!"

Leave your prejudices at the door.

When you meet the Seven Princes, you will recognize males you know—especially any exes—but do not bring your encounters with them into the equation. For example, just because your ex was a Prince 7 and he cheated on you, that doesn't mean all Prince 7s are cheats. *All* these princes are capable of wrongdoing, just as all humans are capable of wrongdoing. Instead, judge them purely on their profiles, not on your prejudicial experiences of their Genetypes.

Don't choose an emotional crutch.

When people say a life partner "completes them," some confusion exists. A loving relationship is something humans need, so yes, having one provides a sense of completion. But when you declare you need another person so you can feel complete, you're saying you aren't complete as an individual. Of course, many people actually *aren't* complete because they have issues to work through (who doesn't?). *But you cannot truly love another until you love yourself.* We'll address that in Part Three, but until then, don't choose the prince you think could "fix" you. He doesn't complete you; you complete yourself. Otherwise, he's not a partner; he's an emotional crutch.

Also, opposites may attract, but that doesn't mean you should make a choice purely on a type you deem is opposite of you—that is, someone who will "balance" you. Remember, you're looking for *compatibility* in life every single day, forever and ever.

Push the star charts to one side.

When I began the research into Genetypes, I was keen to find any link between them and zodiac signs but found none—not even close. So, saying things like, "Oh, he's a Capricorn, and I would *never* date a Capricorn" can deprive you of what could be your ideal match. Plus, when you ask guys what star sign they are (usually within the first ten seconds of first contact), most of them think, "Oh, God, here we go. If I'm not the right sign, she won't take this any further."

Why would you make potential suitors feel like they're being (unnecessarily) tested before you've had a chance to know them? Now isn't the time to get into a big discussion about astrology (and I don't preclude its validity), but the prophecies star signs make are extremely broad. If a certain person's sign doesn't fit the required narrative, the believer usually blames it on "being on the cusp" or similar lingo.

Most of all, it appears that dating by star signs hasn't worked out for you so far.

Leave Daddy out of it.

People say that women often marry their father—not literally, of course, but figuratively in that the husband shows similarities with his wife's father. Don't make this mistake. This idea is clearly a function of nurture and has nothing to do with compatibility. If you've always known your father, you will see him in the lineup of Seven Princes, which is something to note for later. But do not choose a prince because he's the same type as your father. Nor should you disqualify his Genetype, either. You want to be *compatible* with a life partner, so be objective.

Furthermore, if you were underloved by your father, don't fall into the trap of choosing the prince who would represent a "bad boy" to you, simply because that behavior feels familiar. (See "Don't choose an emotional crutch.")

Consider the "fault line."

Too many people, especially young people, think they're compatible because of trivial commonalities. "He likes Scrabble, and so do I!

And, guess what? He loves Yorkshire terriers *and so do I!*' Spooky. Having shared interests provides kindling fuel for the fire, but regard that as a bonus. Instead, carefully scan for the relationship "fault line" —an inherent potential flashpoint based on fundamental differences. Note: Every couple has a fault line as a result of their inherent nature, and it has nothing to do with male-female differences.

Realize that a relationship "fault line" becomes an earthquake under pressure. (Having children, for example, is a great source of pressure.) As you're selecting, vividly imagine that kind of scenario with each of these princes as a simulation of inevitable life challenges you must *meet together as a team.*

Be aware of the two sides to our nature—light and dark. They exist in all types and in all things as a law of the Universe. Noting a prince's "darkness" in the descriptions that follow will help you consider the fault line you'd have as a couple. But because there is also light within the darkness, try to see the good in him. And if both parties are mindful of the "fault line," the two of you can survive any earthquake.

Identify and discard deal-breakers.

Take a piece of paper and draw a line down the middle. On one side, write YES, and on the other side write NO. Remember that, objectively speaking, no perfect prince exists. Princes all have good and bad points. This exercise provides guidance on deciding what is a YES or a NO for *you.*

As you read through the descriptions of the Seven Princes, the deal-breakers should quickly stand out, so put those profiles in the NO column and add the profiles you like to the YES column. Use a pencil so you can make the inevitable changes as you carefully re-consider. As much as anything, it's a process of deduction, so think about it this way: If you've identified three or four definite NOs, that's 50 percent fewer frogs you'll have to kiss!

Remember, it's okay and normal to have multiple YESes. Ideally, you choose one, but it's not essential at this time, as I'll explain. Right now, you're after the *likelihood* of compatibility.

Using me with female Genetypes as an example, my piece of paper would have five NOs and two YESes. That means I could leave myself open to being in a relationship with either one of the YESes, which provides better odds to the chance of finding the best chemistry. The deciding factors might include how severe their Genetypal flaws have evolved. (With experience and/or maturity, people usually mellow out and become more mindful of their flaws. Conversely, those flaws can be exacerbated over time. More about this in Part Five.)

Look at the totality of the man.

Don't write the guy off as a NO based on the first aspect of him you dislike. As you read the profiles carefully, consider each as a "sum of the parts" that make him the prince he is, with all his ingrained and interlinked traits stemming from what drives him (his Dominant Driver).

And now, it's time to choose from Seven Princes on the menu, but let me first explain the rules of the house.

Rules of the House

Choose a dish or go hungry.

Please only choose from the menu of the Seven Princes. It's not a la carte; it's table d'hôte with a fixed menu and pricing—that is, only these choices are available. *Nurture* is merely the toppings on the main dish of *nature*; you can add sauce to a steak, but it's still a steak.

No substitutions.

Important point: *I didn't make up these profiles; they simply exist, so don't shoot the messenger.* I've done this for years now, and I kept going because of my passion and dedication to something that's incredibly real. So, "as it comes" is the only way you get the dish. That means you can't switch out the parts you don't like, and don't pout when you get confirmation that Prince Perfect doesn't exist. It isn't my fault that "this one guy would be *sooo* perfect if he didn't xyz!"

Yet, although you can't change him, you can help him become more mindful of his flaws if you handle feedback in a constructive way and reinforce it with love and support (as Part Seven will show). Age and experience will naturally mellow out his flaws. Having said that, true love is *unconditional* love, which means working with reality, not fantasy. So, suck it up. *No substitutions!*

Tasting menu available.

As stated, you can choose more than one dish, but only as a sample. Ultimately, you'll have to select only one. But sampling IS allowed and encouraged!

With these rules firmly in mind, please, be our guest.

Table d'hôte Menu

Tasting notes:

- Next to each prince title, you'll notice a blank space. You're asked to assign a nickname to each one as a memory tag. Thus, when you think of a prince's nickname, eventually you can quickly remember the profile in question, so try to think of a suitable name after you've studied the profile. (Note: You'll have only your one-to-three YES profiles to remember.) Making it personal to you has more meaning than if I assigned nicknames for you, and you'll need these nicknames in Part Five.

- If you're a *The You Code* reader looking for a correlation between the Genetypes and princes, know that the numbers match (e.g., MG-1 = Prince 1, MG-2 = Prince 2, etc.), although I advise you to treat this book in isolation.

- Each prince's Dominant Driver represents his single most defining characteristic. It's the trunk of the tree that feeds all other branches of behavior.

- Server's Suggestions (my opinions) are shown for each. Act as you would if a restaurant server made a menu suggestion for you—listen but make your own decision. I offer the type of woman that is probably well suited or not well suited for each prince, using a simple phrase to best define that type of woman as follows: Nurturer, Problem Solver, Spiritual and Sensitive to Energy, Spontaneous and Passionate, Fights for Equality, Childlike Healer, and Champion of Family Values. See if any of these ring true for you, purely as a guide. The type of woman matched with any given prince is not necessarily a reflection on the prince. For example, matching a certain prince with a woman who says she's spiritual doesn't necessarily mean the prince in question is also spiritual. If a certain type of woman isn't mentioned in the Server's Suggestions, then the server is neutral.

Prince 1: _____ (your nickname)

OVERVIEW:

He's a career man. He's strategic, a logical planner, and a team player. A map of cause and effect guides his path, making the game of life seem obvious to him. Many people focus on their professional lives, but for him, it *is* his life—and happily so. Being focused and driven makes him adept at accomplishing goals but more comfortable as a manager, freelancer, or professional rather than going all the way to being owner/CEO of a corporation/organization. The perfect wingman, he's a loyal senior manager who acts as if the organization he works for is his own. He sets the bar high for himself and others, which makes him the employee organizational leaders dream about. He's why they invented the Rolodex, and he's likely to take his business cards on vacation. Smart, orderly, and wise.

DOMINANT DRIVER:

Logic

GREATEST ASSET FOR RELATIONSHIPS:

Dependability

BIGGEST DISLIKES:

- Chaos, lack of structure and routine
- Failing at work, losing respect from colleagues

- Emotions, dealing with overemotional people
- Retirement, stillness

THE LIGHT:

This is a safe-and-steady man who takes responsibility seriously, including marriage and family life. People look up to him at work, and his superiors respect him. He can be competitive in a calm and healthy way. He integrates and blends with a team. When faced with a situation, family members are reminded of how he can be counted on, always there for them with the wisdom of Solomon, keen to assist with his skills and knowledge.

THE DARKNESS:

The biggest dark side aspect is his arrogance. He can also be stubborn and pompous at times. Being married to his career can make his partner feel more like a mistress and, if he's not mindful, make his children see him as a distant uncle. Romantically, he can lack spontaneity and passion, be somewhat withdrawn and robotic, and find it difficult to express emotions (the opposite of logic).

SERVER'S SUGGESTIONS:

Well suited for: *Problem Solver, Champion of Family Values, Nurturer.*

Least suited for: *Spiritual and Sensitive to Energy, Spontaneous and Passionate, Fights for Equality, Childlike Healer.*

Prince 2: _____ (your nickname)

OVERVIEW:

He's an intellectual. Driven by a need for knowledge and understanding of the world, he requires solitude to be alone with his
thoughts. The more he knows of the world, the more he feels the
need to withdraw from it. The drama, the hypocrisy, the brutality,
the superficiality—it appalls him. His home is his castle, his
laboratory, his watchtower, his bunker, and where he wants to spend
most of his time. He's an interesting, knowledgeable man you can
have deep conversations with. In what might seem a contradiction,
he can also be a spiritual person who is aware of other dimensions.
Some people might see him as an endearing eccentric.

DOMINANT DRIVER:

Knowledge

GREATEST ASSET FOR RELATIONSHIPS:

Deep conversation. Space (if required).

BIGGEST DISLIKES:

• Living among "the masses" and as one of them

• Loss of home and solitude

• Invasion of privacy, socially and legally

THE LIGHT:

Multiple layers of knowledge and skill can reveal a charming renais-
sance man if you're allowed access to his rich inner sanctum. He has
a wonderful curiosity and appetite for adventure; he's happy to leave
his home to travel to strange new lands, to learn and explore. He
senses there is something else out there, perhaps other dimensions,

and spirituality appeals to his nature. He's an intelligent and particular man who loves to read and live inside his head. Those who are exposed to his philosophies and theories can have their lives changed forever, potentially drawing a great following or even changing the world.

THE DARKNESS:

If some kind of drama forces him to step out of his reclusive lifestyle, he can go on a rampage, surprising those who wrote him off as a timid hermit. He can also struggle to show emotions, and communicating well can be a challenge.

SERVER'S SUGGESTIONS:

Well suited for: *Spiritual and Sensitive to Energy, Childlike Healer.*

Least suited for: *Nurturer, Problem Solver, Champion of Family Values.*

Prince 3:_____ (your nickname)

OVERVIEW:

He's creative with a vivid imagination. If he follows his true purpose in life, he is a creative artist of some kind. A truth-seeker, he likes to disrupt the status quo, indiscriminately challenge any consensus, and wake people up. His eyes say it all: mysterious, intense, and soulful. He senses a connection with energy and other dimensions, and he enjoys nature. He wears his heart on his sleeve with emotions on full display, good or bad. He's sensitive to other people's energy, making him intuitive when required. He can change like the ocean, the beauty making up for the storms. A character like him frequently appears on TV shows because writers tend to write characters based on themselves. On any given day, this type of male can be anything from a brooding Don Draper (*Mad Men*) to a playful Hank Moody (*Californication*) to a curmudgeonly Larry David (*Curb Your Enthusiasm*). Never a dull moment.

DOMINANT DRIVER:

Creativity

GREATEST ASSET FOR RELATIONSHIPS:

Romance and passion

BIGGEST DISLIKES:

- Criticism

- Writer's block (if in a creative job)

- Monotony

THE LIGHT:

His changing moods coupled with an inherent need to break monotony keeps life colorful. Romantic, passionate, and spontaneous, he is one of your best bets for the "flowers and candlelit dinner" guy. If you enjoy the arts, this is your man for theater and galleries, plus he can indiscriminately appreciate any kind of art form, even old romantic movies. On a good day, he can be the heart of a party or a night out. For him, variety is the spice of life. You'll have no complaints if you're looking for a man who will tell you how he feels.

THE DARKNESS:

Changing moods coupled with an inherent need to break monotony can be unnecessarily destructive, also making him unpredictable. He can be solemn in mood, dragging others down with him. He can be unnecessarily jealous. He's not always in control of his emotions, the bad as well as the good, and can say the things most people think but know not to say. (Saying what we think instead of biting our tongue is the underlying premise of *Curb Your Enthusiasm*.) Sensitive to criticism, he can be self-centered. His creative nature may have been buried by ego and societal pressure.

SERVER'S SUGGESTIONS:

Well suited for: *Spiritual and Sensitive to Energy, Spontaneous and Passionate, Childlike Healer.*

Least suited for: *Problem Solver, Nurturer.*

Prince 4:_____ (your nickname)

OVERVIEW:

He's a smooth-talking gentleman who loves to party, a hedonist, and a nonconformist. Being immune to society's pressure on males to gain wealth and success brings him occasional disdain from men, but women are his preferred company anyway. Women fascinate him; he sees beauty in some form in *all* women, almost to the point of worshipping them. Just because he relates to women so well doesn't mean he isn't masculine inside and out; that has nothing to do with gender or sexual preference. Sensitive to energy, he can see into women's hearts, as other women can, and as a result, he's often told he's psychic.

DOMINANT DRIVER:

Philosophy (but he often doesn't know it)

GREATEST ASSET FOR RELATIONSHIPS:

Empathy. Sexual exploration.

BIGGEST DISLIKES:

- Males seeing him as inferior, effeminate, or a "loser"

- Hard work and conforming

- Being deprived of life's pleasures

THE LIGHT:

He's great to talk to, fun to be around, and often found laughing among a huddle of women at any party. He emboldens women and raises their self-esteem. His affinity and fascination with women make him naturally do something most other males can't or won't do: *he listens to them.*

THE DARKNESS:

He's sensitive, and that can make him changeable and suffer from mood swings, although he's always kind and gentle with women. He doesn't follow rules happily, and some find that frustrating. He's not a career man, but he knows the life that wealth could give him. Thus, he can be inclined to bounce from one failed scheme to the next, struggling to find his purpose in life. His love of women—and how they love him back—can increase any risk of infidelity *if* he's not satisfied in a relationship. Others, men especially, can see him as a dropout and an anarchist.

SERVER'S SUGGESTIONS:

Well suited for: *Spiritual and Sensitive to Energy, Spontaneous and Passionate, Fights for Equality.*

Least suited for: *Problem Solver, Champion of Family Values.*

Prince 5: _____ (your nickname)

OVERVIEW:

He's forever young, carefree, and cocky, and if others want to grow up, that's their problem. Their boring life is something they're reminded of when others come to him. He's a great friend to unwind or find where the party is. He pranks, plays, and encourages others to loosen up. He has little interest in the trappings of life, because that's exactly what they are to him: *trap*pings. Life is supposed to be fun, and he dresses accordingly. The world is his playground, and children gravitate toward him because of it. In fact, he has retained many aspects of his childhood, while others lost them as they entered adulthood. A child is innocent, curious, loving, and fun, and so is Prince 5.

DOMINANT DRIVER:

Freedom

GREATEST ASSET FOR RELATIONSHIPS:

Having fun, needing space (if required).

BIGGEST DISLIKES:

- Total loss of freedom, space, and alone time
- Being tied down and trapped
- Boredom, monotony, hard work, wearing suits or uniforms, and working in rigidly structured environments

THE LIGHT:

He has the wonderful imagination and curiosity of a child, infectious enthusiasm, playfulness, and excessive boldness. He can be charmingly mischievous, eavesdropping, and storytelling, living in a fun-filled fantasy world. A risk-taker, he possesses a youthful sense of invincibility, parading through life like a superhero.

THE DARKNESS:

When it comes to communicating, he can appear distracted, somewhere else, with a blank look on his face, and this can be frustrating. He's not good at making major decisions, thus he needs guidance. The good traits of a child are paired with a child's less desirable traits: potentially being amoral, flighty, and entitled. Commitment represents a threat to his freedom.

SERVER'S SUGGESTIONS:

Well suited for: *Nurturer, Spiritual and Sensitive to Energy, Spontaneous and Passionate.*

Least suited for: *Problem Solver, Champion of Family Values* (yet, interestingly, these two types of women often marry this prince for all the wrong reasons: they see a man who is easy to control/ dominate).

Prince 6:_____ (your nickname)

OVERVIEW:

He's physical, a fist-bumping "man's man." In the moment, in his body, in the fight, he cares little for tomorrow or career. He is a fearless protector who will readily take up a cause, sucking up life's joys as they present themselves, feasting and partying as if tomorrow is the last day on earth. Fiery, he walks through life on a knife edge, scanning for danger, sometimes secretly wishing he could spring into action and mercilessly test his bodily skills. He's a literal man—what you see is what you get—and life is simple for him. He's passionate, spontaneous, and drawn to danger. He enjoys "rescuing" women who like to be "rescued." Most males loved Han Solo in *Star Wars*, and he identified with Hans Solo most. As Han Solo said, "I prefer a straight fight to all this sneaking around."

DOMINANT DRIVER:

Protecting

GREATEST ASSET FOR RELATIONSHIPS:

Physical security and protection. Spontaneity.

BIGGEST DISLIKES:

- Failing at defending those he loves
- Losing any battle, especially physical
- Being a corporate "drone"

THE LIGHT:

If having a protector watch over you is your priority, then this is your guy. Drama doesn't bother him like it does others; he loves answering an emergency call. His house is the wrong house to break into; it would be a truly bad day for the invader. His simplicity and singularity mean you always know what you're getting without layers of complexity or duality to fathom. He's a spontaneous man who will thrive with a spontaneous partner. If you need the thrill of the chase, then he's all over it.

THE DARKNESS:
He can seem on edge, taking things too literally and overreacting, being overly aggressive. He can sometimes appear uncouth, thick-headed, and animalistic. Actions are preferable to words, which can cause communication issues. He can fly off the handle easily. People sense his trigger fingers and can quickly intimidate them.

SERVER'S SUGGESTIONS:
Well suited for: *Problem Solver, Spontaneous and Passionate.*

Least suited for: *Spiritual and Sensitive to Energy, Fights for Equality, Nurturer.*

Prince 7: _____ (your nickname)

OVERVIEW:

He's a born leader. This man is a tower of confidence. Multitalented, he's always striving to *be* the best and to *have* the best. He *needs* to be the man in charge, in both his professional and personal life; anything other than first place is abhorrent to him. Anyone who challenges his power or position will incur his displeasure—justifiably so, he believes. He doesn't know how to show emotions and love—he sees that as weakening his power—so he might use gifts to do today's job or a promise of something in the future. He likes to "rule" over a black-and-white world, embracing the finest things in life. On an endless quest to be the best, he often succeeds, thanks to his aptitudes, confidence, and charm. He embraces the idea of not needing to change who he is, because he has no intention of changing.

DOMINANT DRIVER:

Power

GREATEST ASSET FOR RELATIONSHIPS:

Leadership

BIGGEST DISLIKES:

- Being a king without a "crown"; he generally needs money and/or power
- Losing control, losing power
- Disrespect
- Showing emotions; he sees emotions as weakness

THE LIGHT:

You're in the hands of a "captain" who needs a good woman at his side as he strives to guide your ship to greatness. He is generous to those who respect him. Sociable and a great networker, he acts like the mayor of wherever he is at the time. You get all the benefits of a man who is full of confidence and charisma: a rock to lean on, engaging conversation, and a man who takes charge.

THE DARKNESS:

The dark side of confidence is being egotistical. He's never wrong and won't back down. If you need a man to show his emotions, then this is not your guy, because a strong leader would be seen as weak by doing so. He can be patriarchal and domineering. Any bad behavior he exhibits is blamed on other people for provoking him.

SERVER'S SUGGESTIONS:

Well suited for: *Champion of Family Values, Problem Solver.*

Least suited for: *Fights for Equality, Nurturer.*

Your Bill, Madame

No rush, take your time. No need to leave this part until you've made the most important decision of your whole life—your choice of who to spend your remaining years with! Remember, it's okay to sample more than one prince at this stage. The main thing is to have eliminated at least half of the men out there while knowing what those deal-breakers look like. In fact, in Parts Five and Six, you will learn how to quickly spot them.

I hope you can see that each of the Seven Princes is nothing like the others. The beauty is that each type brings a strong asset to the table of romantic relations, and any dark side they have is the associated flip side of their light side—the nature of the beast. Because they're all different, you get to choose based on your biggest long-term priorities and how he aligns with your true nature.

A word of caution: Once you take this knowledge into the real world and meet some of these princes, you will likely see aspects that weren't present before and want to modify your choice(s). Don't be shy to do so. Keep an open mind.

You saw your father in the lineup, didn't you? Take note as you move to the next chapter. Now that you have a clear idea of what your prince(s) looks like, prepare to meet him (them).

But first, enough about princes; let's talk about *you* . . .

part three

WANTED:
Wife Material

Every Time Is the First Time

"Return to the world still more brilliant
because of your former sorrows."

- ALEXANDRE DUMAS, *The Count of Monte Cristo*

Luck is found at the crossroads of opportunity and preparation, so let's spend time on the preparation part. Before we open the gates and let you loose on those princes, let's ensure you bring your A-game. You may *think* you're already bringing it, but maybe it's time to question what you think is your A-game.

Last night at a bar (aka my alternate research lab), I overhead two single women talking. Well, "talking" isn't the right word. It was more like bitching-in-stereo as they simultaneously complained to each other about how hard it is to find a boyfriend and how all the guys they've dated have either been "losers" or "assholes." I wondered how sore their jaws would be after this high-speed venting match —an impressive display.

On the other side of the bar were two great-looking, well-behaved guys, God love them, who were trying to make eye contact with the two women with machine-gun mouths. Definitely not a "Hooya!" moment for these ladies.

"Well," you might ask, "why didn't those guys just walk over and introduce themselves?" Seriously? Even Prince 6 wouldn't have the balls to step into that crossfire. (In Part Six, we'll chat about how it's supposedly easy for a guy to "just walk over.")

After the two women had dumped what they needed to, they paused for breath, giggled at what they'd just said, snatched a half-hearted sip of their now-warm martinis, and flickered their eyes around the room in the sly way one does when scanning for prospects. By then, the two guys had left for a different bar, seeking women who would pay attention to them and, most of all, who were not *prisoners of their pasts*.

Your "Titanic" may well have hit an iceberg in the past, but that's where it remains: *in the past*. By far, the most common issue with single women is sheer unwillingness, yes *unwillingness*, to let go of the past and the prejudices it creates. Thus, they sink any new opportunity, clinging to their pain as if it's a lifesaver when it's actually a life-destroyer. They judge and blame all men in the present based on their past, never once looking in the mirror. When I confront my female clients with this truth, they frequently say, "I know . . . I really *know*." And that's the problem right there; stop "knowing" by using your head, and start *feeling* by using your *heart*. Treat every new romantic experience as what it is: *new*, like sailing into every dawn as a fresh adventure to be grateful for.

Stop staring at the shipwreck,
and instead notice the undiscovered country
it brought you to.

If you've loved, you've lived. *And you've felt pain.* Yet we tend to associate that pain with the experience that caused it—forever. Evolutionary psychology has an explanation for this: it's simply about survival. Most of human behavior can be related to seeking pleasure and avoiding pain. Our brains are hardwired to associate pain with experiences, so we can learn lessons such as "fire will burn you."

Recall that for more than 99 percent of human existence, we were living in the wild with the rest of the animal kingdom. That means, in these modern times, our brains haven't evolved fast enough to keep up with our contemporary need to *consciously* discern between the "experience-pain tags" we *should* place on incidents (such as "fire will burn you") and the tags we *shouldn't* place (such as "men will burn you").

This ancient programming works against you in relationships, so become mindful of it. *Healthy (not debilitating) fear* served as an essential survival tool for primitive humans, but in this relatively new and safe age:

Fear prevents life more
than it prevents death.

Primal fear automatically makes us avoid what we *perceive* are the consequences of past pain, which stops us moving in a desired direction. Fears are rarely based on real risk—only the risk we perceive. (I feel a workbook-ish moment coming on . . .)

Now, take a piece of paper and write down all your deepest relationship fears, then relate each fear to a particular relationship experience you've had. Don't use the blank pages in this book. You'll soon see why.

Are all your fears and associated memories now listed on that piece of paper? Great. Wasn't it interesting to see how many of these relationship fears are born of prejudices related to past relationships? Lovely.

Now, burn that piece of paper. Use the most dramatic instrument you can find, ideally a flame thrower, a Molotov cocktail, or taped to a firework rocket. Aren't you glad you didn't use this book to write on? Give it time, though. You're not through with this chapter yet, and your demons are already gunning for me . . .

Keep repeating this paper exercise until the only thing written on that piece of paper is this:

[INTENTIONALLY LEFT BLANK]

Only then can you put your matches away. If you're about to write your own fairy tale, then become what all writers both dread and dream about: The Blank Page. This is the blank page you were born with. You must return to that pure state, to the Mother Ship, the source. Yes, making your romantic journey a continual blank page makes you vulnerable. That's why writers both dread and dream about The Blank Page: because it takes courage to embrace your vulnerability, to stand up in front of everyone and say:

"Look! Here is my heart and soul! Feel free to stomp all over it. But, unless you're up here on the stage with me, I couldn't give a damn what you think, for every day brings a brand-new performance for me to embrace."

Let yourself feel vulnerable, step into it, *feel* your heart pound (instead of texting its emoji to everyone). To love with no guarantee of it being reciprocated is vulnerability, but if you want a guarantee, well, buy a toaster. Life doesn't come with guarantees, least of all love. You roll with the punches. Maybe you win, maybe you lose. At least you now have a pulse, and you're playing in the game called "life."

Adversity has always been the staging post of a human's finest hour. Having existed for 2.5 million years because we are inherent winners, humans are built to strive and *win*. You are not genetically designed to shiver in the shadows. Make every time the *first* time instead of leaving your soul frozen to your past.

Let It Go

If you've fallen through the ice, you'll drown unless you can see where you fell in, so let's identify that hole you fell through and climb out of it. Better still, let's make sure you stop walking on thin ice in the first place.

Please read all of my open letters that follow, even if they don't apply to you, because there's a lesson in each. None of these lessons involve telling you what you want to hear, blowing smoke, or trying to make me look like a nice guy.

• • •

Dear Divorcee,

I've been divorced twice, and I've walked in your shoes. So, who the hell am I to be giving relationship advice, right? Wrong. It's called *learning the hard way*. When you know what *not* to do, you know what *to* do *if* you can make friends with your past and learn from it.

There is something about a divorce that doesn't compare to a regular breakup. It's like a tear in the fabric of the Universe; it simply wasn't supposed to happen. But it *did*, and depending on the length of the marriage, a full recovery from it can take years, even if you were the one who wanted the divorce. It feels like your life has crashed, and, as in a car accident, you experience mental trauma as you stare at the surreal image of the wreckage. But if you're too busy staring in the rearview mirror, you're going to crash again.

Then the diseases of blame and shame set in, with the symptoms leading nowhere. You are not a failure; rather, you *experienced* failure. You made a mistake, but *you are not stupid*. No singular party is to blame for a divorce; it takes two to make or break it. That's what a marriage is supposed to be—a partnership—and that means *joint* responsibility.

But now, that agreement is dissolved. He doesn't need to forgive you in order for you to move on. You cannot control his actions or inactions; you can only control how you respond or don't respond to them. You are no longer together by legal definition; you're mentally on your own. That's a good thing. It means that, without permission from him, you can take this powerful step: *You will muster your inner strength to unilaterally move forward through the formidable power of forgiveness.*

Forgiveness is the freeway through your grieving process. Whenever you think of him—whatever he did or you believe he did—use your heart instead of your head and send him kind thoughts. Only then can you truly say "goodbye" to him and "hello" to your future.

Knowing his Genetype is a powerful forgiveness tool if you see his actions as his inherent nature and *know this mess wasn't all your fault.* Different female Genetypes respond in different ways to a divorce—ranging from nonchalance to feeling like their DNA has dissolved. (Refer to *The You Code* for seeing how and why you are dealing with it in your own Genetypal way.)

It may not seem like it now, but you *will* love and be loved again—*provided you forgive yourself and believe you deserve to be loved.* Your next relationship won't only benefit from a better partner selection; you will also gain from your life experience in your past marriage. And you'll never make those same relationship mistakes again, right? This time around, you'll be yelling, "Hooya!" all the way up the aisle.

• • •

Dear Dumpee,

Your boyfriend dumped you, and it feels like you swallowed a brick. Even the dumbest thing reminds you of him. It sucks . . . *right now.* Time heals, and the Universe seems to have a funky plan for each of us so things will work out for the better—*if we would only sit up and pay attention to its signs instead of fighting them.*

I say this from long experience—not spiritual mumbo-jumbo or happy-clappy handouts—but by realizing this for myself. It's time to trust in a higher power and pay attention to where it's taking you. Reading this book was probably part of the mysterious and grand plan of the Universe, especially if you can now see your ex-boyfriend's Genetype and realize you weren't a match anyway. What if his Genetype *was* a match for you? Great news: the Universe cloned the SOB!

Remember, where it counts—compatibility—he is only one of seven in a clone army. You're now free to find "him" (your prince) again. Who knows, maybe this version might clean up after himself and do everything better this time.

I hope you can learn something from the previous letter to divorcees. If nothing else, you can see you're more fortunate this happened now and not later on. Things do happen for a reason, good or bad, and when you accept that events are ultimately and mysteriously working for you, everything changes.

If you aren't failing, you aren't trying. Failing lets you overcome fear because you're now dealing with reality instead of your imagined fantasy of what failure might have looked like. Take some bizarre solace from that!

Be happy and choose right; the Universe always has a plan up its sleeve.

• • •

Dear Single Mom,

For you, I'll keep it short and sweet. Do you know what's really unattractive about single moms? *When they try to conceal that fact.*

Listen, if the word "baggage" is so much as a fleeting thought from you or anyone in your vicinity, I'll jump off this page and slap whoever is responsible. Don't dare think for a second that your beautiful children aren't anything other than gifts to the world.

You have the power to give life, you gave life, and you will be proud of the fact.

Own it, advertise it, laugh loudly at your children's adventures, and pass around the photos. A good guy, a *serious* guy, will like your kids and accept that you have a past. The woman he's about to fall in love with wouldn't be that same woman without those children.

And did you know that single dads exist too? Umm, *hell-o.* Can you say "playdate-cum-margarita-mix-off"? Kids are inadvertently great dating event organizers (but train them to filter out the dads with wedding rings). Many men, mostly those with children, are relieved if your need to reproduce has been satisfied; it means they don't have to relive the trauma of changing diapers at three in the morning. (Personally, the thought of going through that again makes my left eye twitch.)

Families don't have to be blended, so don't let that put you off. Don't plan too far ahead. Just focus on your children without letting their existence prevent you from having a love life *and* without hiding them in the attic.

• • •

Dear Mature Woman,

I get it. I too hug the liquor store cashier on the rare occasions that they ask to check my ID. But maturing doesn't mean giving up. I was sitting at a bar the other night (yes, *again*, research for this book created a legitimate tax write-off for vodka consumption, okay?) and saw that loved-up elderly couple described in Part One there. Probably in their late seventies, they were stroking and feeding each other, the whole shebang. They sat still and mellow, enjoying the live music.

Then, the live band played a rap song from the nineties, and suddenly, the elderly lady unleashed her long, white hair and danced her heart out while her husband cheered on her "let-me-show-you-dumb-kids-how-it's-done" moves. It was as surreal as it was wonderful. Most of all, in that moment, *she was the coolest girl in the room.*

Men who were young enough to be her son or grandson abandoned their conversations with their partners to watch her, and I don't mean in a shocked or scornful way. Please know this: your body is passing, but your soul is eternal, and . . .

When we fall in love, we fall in love with a person's soul.

I hate clichés, especially when they're true, but a person's age truly is "just a number"—a legal label on a piece of paper. Your truer age is your biometric age, a function of your health. Note the lessons here for all ages. For example, that dancing lady had the courage to be vulnerable and not care what anyone thought; *she respected herself* more than anyone watching her.

• • •

Dear Mirror-Smasher,

There's a reason why Amazon's chain of retail stores is called "Four Star" and not "Five Star." It's the same reason research shows that people are suspicious of five-star ratings, and that four-star-rated products usually perform better. And that reason is:

Imperfection is what makes us human.

Media messages would have you believe otherwise, even if it means having teeth so ludicrously perfect that you look like a cartoon character. I once had a date with a girl who had one front incisor tooth that visibly stuck out. But there was a good reason I'd asked her on a date, which led to a wonderful relationship. When I had first met her, of course I noticed her tooth, and I thought it was kind of cute, but she didn't know that. She did the best thing she could've done—she pointed out her crooked tooth. Better still, she made a joke about it by attempting to push it back into alignment with her fingers, and I almost fell in love with her on the spot because of it.

Laughing at ourselves makes us irresistibly attractive
to another person's soul, because
it's the antithesis of ego. Ego only cares about
the superficial; it's not what we fall in love with.

That is why adults instinctively smile at children or animals; they regard them as pure beings devoid of ego. That woman had so much character, charm, wit, and courage that every one of her teeth could've been crooked for all I cared. Maybe you don't think you possess charm or wit, but that doesn't matter, because what was most attractive about her was this:

She didn't walk around with a cloud over her head
because of how she felt about herself.
She respected herself enough to laugh at herself,
at her imperfections, and I could either take it
or leave it. I chose to take it, with both hands.

Women have often shared their "wisdom" with me about what women want—"deep secrets" such as "we want a man who can make us laugh . . . and a man who is confident." Thanks for the scoop, ladies, but what makes you think that's singular to women? Too much has been made about the differences between men and women. Apart from some primal differences we'll talk about later, this "mystery" about men (or women, for that matter) isn't much more than the Genetype profiles already shown. Those profiles exposed the inherent weaknesses of all men—that they are clearly *imperfect*—so why would they even *want* you to be perfect?

For most of human existence, survival had a better chance by being part of a tribe. That meant not being rejected by a tribe, which was pretty much a death sentence. *So, humans are programmed to conform.* When you're exposing yourself to a contrived "consensus" about how looking like an airbrushed, makeup-caked celebrity will make you feel valued (to the "tribe"), you unconsciously compare yourself to this image. Consequently, you judge your self-worth incorrectly.

Instead, seize the courage to be imperfect. Muster the compassion to be kinder to yourself. Be authentic—be who you want to be. And stop gazing at glossy images, letting others tell you what's "cool." What's actually "cool" is not giving a crap about what's cool. It's your spirit, confidence, character, and other attractive qualities saying, "I love myself enough to have a mind of my own, thank you very much." *Those are the words of a woman who is irresistibly attractive.*

Realize the world is a mirror reflecting back all your emotions. If you think you're unworthy, unlovable, and deserving of struggle, the world will treat you that way. Although you aren't aware of it, you project how you feel onto people and situations. This kind of attitude is dating-world suicide, *so cut it out.*

• • •

Dear Inner Child,

Think for a minute what your family's expectations of you were. Parents have their own dreams, too. Often, they try to live life again through their children and have no idea the damage they're doing, because children have a natural and innocent desire to please their parents. Let's not assign blame to anyone. Raising kids has to be the most important and demanding task ever to fall on an individual's shoulders. In grade school, you're taught how to solve a simultaneous equation and observe the painfully obvious fact that water evaporates when you heat it. But not once is the most important task you'd ever confront even mentioned.

You had a dominant male influence in your childhood, probably your father, and saw his profile among the princes. (If you didn't, go back and take an honest look.) Your relationship with that profile as a child created your mental model for how males should/could treat you in later life. (See your mother's profile in *The You Code*. It reveals her influence on you about how a woman should act. This may also explain any clashes with her.) The father-daughter dynamic may now make more sense when you see your father as just another male Genetype, especially if his influence on you was related to his inherent nature. This also means *you'll be able to separate from the synthetic programming of your nurture, good or bad.* That synthetic programming is sometimes referred to as your "inner child." Yes, the "child" is always with you, but you don't have to be a slave to its tantrums. Be mindful, which is partly the ability to discern between what your inner child wants you to do and what your sense of right or wrong—your gut, your true spirit—wants you to do.

Only you can know who your inner child is and how she influences you, but I do know this: there is a "deleted scene" in your biography, a painful event in childhood that was covered up in your memory. When you remember it, you'll understand that child inside you.

• • •

This crucial postscript with its common denominator applies to all these open letters:

> P.S. *It is virtually IMPOSSIBLE to fall in love with a woman who does not respect herself. To fall in love with someone, you need to respect that person, so how can you respect someone who doesn't respect themselves?*

Therefore, you can't fast track your fairy tale ending unless you've got that part down.

Next, let's put concrete steps in place to help you project an image of self-respect on the dating scene while seizing every advantage that might put you with your chosen prince. I'm done with the hugging; let's proceed with the shaking.

The WANTED Woman

*"Pour yourself a drink, put on some lipstick,
and pull yourself together."*
– ELIZABETH TAYLOR

Perception is reality. If you're *perceived* as wanted, then you *are* wanted. I don't want to change you; I want you to step into the best version of you by remembering you need to be WANTED:

Womanly

Assertive

Naughty

Tasteful

Entertained

Dignified

Don't pull out the rosary beads at the sight of "Naughty"; I'll go over each of these items to explain. Note that being caring and supportive to a partner isn't listed because it's a "given" with someone you love. Nothing on this WANTED list requires changing your basic nature, but some will come more naturally to certain female Genetypes than others. For example, some women are "duh!" about being Womanly while others are "duh!" about being Assertive. However, *everything* on the WANTED list is within you, either from nature, experience, or simply lying dormant. What's important to remember, like it or not, is this:

♛

The kind of man you want to attract
has all these requirements.

The underlying requirement in WANTED—the base of the recipe —is confidence, defined as "the state of feeling certain about the truth of something." That "something" is identifying *precisely* what you want *and* knowing your chosen prince better than he knows himself. Therefore, you have confidence, at least when it comes to the matter in question. This knowledge is your ace card that empowers you as you walk in any room. It's the voltage behind the energy you give off, the truth that cuts through the cloud of uncertainty that hangs over everyone else. Knowledge is power, power is confidence, and confidence is the foundation of a WANTED woman.

"W" Is for Womanly

Just as women are attracted to masculinity, men are attracted to femininity. Once you've found him, feel free to stay indoors wearing matching sweatpants, but at least until then, it's time to make an effort. This doesn't mean you have to join the circus and put on more makeup than a clown plus wear heels as high as stilts. It's your version of femininity you need to bring out.

Can you hear that sound? It's me walking on eggshells. It's time to introduce you to a third party who is joining you and me on this mission . . .

Contemporary society applauds what it calls "real talk" but complains when so-called "real talk" doesn't match what it wishes to be real. So, to cater to this blatant hypocrisy, I've invited the Speech Police (aka my editor, Barbara) to carefully monitor everything I say. Every time I appear to bust "the speech limit," the Speech Police will pull me over and ask me to qualify and justify what I'm saying. I chose an avatar for the Speech Police that I think won't trigger anyone. Speak of the devil, I see flashing red-and-blue lights, hear muffled radio chatter . . .

"STOP! SPEECH POLICE."

"Yes, officer?"

"This avatar you chose could be seen as a bit sexist to women."

My response: "This is a dating book designed for best results, so it deals with how the world is, not how you want the world to be. For discussions on how the world *should* be, that's in a different section of the bookstore.

This avatar isn't slutty; she's just feminine, and there's a reason. *Men are highly visual.* Of course, women are visual too, but mostly up to the point of first contact. Then they naturally shift priorities beyond the visual (such as "great, let's see if this guy can string a sentence together"), whereas a man may not. Often, he happily proceeds with the interaction and never moves beyond visuals. (You'll understand why in Part Four.) I suggest you accentuate your womanly appearance to your advantage. Smoke-and-mirrors tactics can distract a man indefinitely as you naturally go beyond visuals and assess if he's your chosen prince while his guard is down. (You will learn to use this advantage in Parts Five and Six when calibrating your basic instinct to your own needs.)

Half-assed efforts deserve *and get* half-assed results. If you want to win, then *play to win.* Listen carefully to everything I'm telling you, safe in the knowledge that the Speech Police are there to protect and serve.

Remember, it's *your own version* of Womanly you want to step into as long as your womanly features are accentuated. You know that girl who walks in the bar, oozing femininity and pheromone, and the heads of both sexes turn in her catlike wake? Yes, *that* girl, the one most other women glare daggers into while their partners' tongues roll out. Well, instead of glaring daggers, you might want to swallow your pride and make a friend of her. She'd be happy to help if you struggle with Womanly. Despite appearances, and unless provoked, she isn't a "bitch" or a "slut." I bet she'd love to bring out your "inner goddess," which is part of her purpose in life (many are beauticians). And if *you* are "that girl," I'm sure you'll back up what I'm saying *and* help your sisters if they call on you.

A Message to Gay People

It's time to say something to the gay and transgender community. I think it's great how our society is progressing with people more willingly accepting others' journeys in life. You won't find anyone who believes in personal liberty more firmly than I do, including the liberty of people to live how they want and to be free from persecution. Here, for the sake of brevity, I make certain assumptions, the main one being that you, the reader, is a female who identifies as a woman with a sexual preference of males. But there's no reason why *anyone* seeking a male partner cannot benefit from this book, including gay males. You simply make your own mental adaptations. (Let me know how it goes. I truly want to help as many people as possible!)

Additionally, I also know finding a partner is a numbers game (and I aim for maximum success rates), so I humbly suggest if you're a female who identifies as a man with a sexual preference of men, you may want to talk about your journey after you've gotten to know your chosen partner better. Your call. Note: Genetypes refer to birth-state biology—sex, not gender—so adapt as necessary.

Weight Loss Thoughts

Next, let's step into a maze filled with linguistic landmines: weight loss. Health considerations aside (because health isn't in this book's mandate), you're either happy with your weight or you aren't—with the operative word being *happy*. Walking around with a cloud of depression over you because of your muffin top or thunder thighs (or whatever other insults you throw at the mirror) is way more unattractive than *having* that muffin top or those thunder thighs. Honest truth: some of the most confident girls I've met were also the most overweight, and confidence wins every time. As you'll see in Part Four, when it comes to looks, the primal male eye is unconsciously scanning for hip-to-waist ratios, not overall size. It's more about the curves being in the right places.

If you're *truly* happy with your weight or shape (no deceiving yourself), then great. If you're not, then do something about it (mostly because of your sad moods that repel people). "Oh, but losing weight isn't that simple," you protest. Actually, it is. A revolutionary weight loss system I use has a 100 percent guaranteed success rate: The Eat Less, Exercise More Plan. Give it a whirl; you'll be thrilled with the results. If that's too facetious for you, I've put together additional free weight-loss information for you here: www.JamesSheridan.com/weightloss.

"A" Is for Assertive

"Oh, women love a man who goes after what he wants," say the ladies with the inside secrets about what women want. Once again, who says that's singular to women?

A woman who knows what she wants,
or doesn't want, is coveted.

This statement is particularly applicable to the first sexual encounter waiting period: "I only want to give myself to the right man, and only when the time is right. You could be that man. Let's enjoy watching things progress!" Boom, the velvet rope just went up. Princes now line up for access to the VIP Lounge, and the players get back to the dance floor, to grope and grind The Lost and The Lazy. Having this kind of assertion is not about being snooty, it's not playing games, and it's not being done in a bitchy way. Be sure you understand clearly what the difference is. (More about this in D for Dignified and in Part Four.)

Ambiguity is a waste of all our time; people want to know where they stand. Yet, most people have no clue other than where they're told to stand by government, media, and society (but it saves thinking for themselves). So, a person we naturally admire isn't part of the bleating masses who have no clear idea about what they want and *what steps they'll take to get it*. There's a phrase to add to your vocabulary: "Coming through!"

Now, asserting yourself and what you want doesn't mean you're a Husband-Seeking Missile (HSM). That's as much of a turnoff as a Man-hating Ice Queen (MIQ). There is a difference between acting desperately and knowing what you want in life. In your mind, you have a clear focus on two things: 1) you want a life partner, and 2) you have a shockingly accurate vision of what that life partner looks like from the prince profiles. The second point especially can make you Assertive. This goal stays in your mind, empowering your every move. But you don't go around saying, "I'm looking for marriage; how about you?" You'd be amazed how many women say that either on or before the first date, and it terrifies a lot of men, even if they have the same goal. I get it. This is stated by a woman who doesn't want to waste her time, not a woman who is asking to get married that night. But it's a clumsy attempt at being Assertive that makes you sound like an HSM. (We'll talk about the right way to go about this in Parts Five and Six.)

It's not that most people *don't* assert themselves in life; it's that they *can't*. They don't know what they're trying to assert, and/or they're not sure they would truly want it even if they did have any idea about it. With relationships, given the knowledge you've gleaned from this book, you've got a clear idea about what you want, and that *automatically* makes you Assertive. Practice asserting yourself in daily life, also, by not putting up with things you don't like or agree with and not being swayed by friends to do things against your will. Politely send back a dish in a restaurant if it's not as you ordered it, or ask your boss for a raise or simply change your job.

Assert yourself. Stand up and be counted by knowing what you truly want, which is more than half the battle. Being Assertive gets you ahead in all matters, not just romantically. (You'll find my best tips on this at www.JamesSheridan.com/goals.)

"N" Is for Naughty

"Naughty" is strictly reserved for the lucky man in your sights, and it does *not* mean slutty or promiscuous. There are two levels of this concept. The first comes naturally to most female types, but some—usually those who are naturally assertive—struggle with it. Highly assertive female types are often successful businesswomen who have difficulty separating their professional life from their personal life. At this first level, Naughty is the glint in your eye that says, "This isn't networking, this is a boy-girl thing, and I like you in a sexual way, okay?" And your conversation should match your intent.

The second level of Naughty requires the most mindfulness. Conveying Naughty at this level says, "I am a sexual woman on a sexual journey, a journey I could be sharing with you." You aren't saying you've been around the block a few times, or that you have a great collection of whips and ball-gags. Rather, you're saying you want to know more; you're open to experimentation in an intimate sense, and he could be the man for the job.

The bottom line of Naughty is this: "If a guy merely wants a room-mate, he'll put an ad on Craigslist."

"T" Is for Tasteful

Hot on the heels of "Naughty" is "Tasteful." The kind of serious guy you want is imagining how it would go down if he introduced you to his friends and family, to his work colleagues, etc. I don't expect you to act like you're in an episode of *Downton Abbey*, sipping your tea with a pinkie finger raised. But understand the standards you should have for yourself in order to be taken seriously by a quality man.

This one is hard to measure, because taste is subjective. Different types of people have different standards, although some basic standards are universal. For example, in some countries, burping and slurping are signs of respect for the host, but in America, most people find such behavior rude.

I once dated a girl who seemed to tick all the boxes until we got to the second date. That's when she explained how she was going to "Dutch Oven" me (meaning she was going to fart in bed and then hold my head under the covers to make me smell it). I'm sure some men would have laughed, but I couldn't get past it. An otherwise promising relationship screeched to a grinding halt, leaving me wondering if the restaurant restrooms had a suitable window I could jump out of. Some things could be mistakenly perceived as intimacy when, in fact, they are simply gross. Maybe you grew up with ten brothers or maybe your parents didn't correct you. But quality men don't care; when it comes to a *life partner*, they simply want a woman who is Tasteful. A gentleman deserves a lady, and a lady deserves a gentleman.

You might say, "Well, I'll be who I am, and he can take it or leave it." You're welcome to do so, but if you're not acting in a tasteful manner *at least in the early stages*, a serious and good man will indeed "leave it." Of course, nobody is born with bad taste; it's acquired through nurture. So, cut through it and *choose* to be a classy lady.

"E" Is for Entertained

I almost wrote "Independent" instead of "Entertained," but if I had spelled "WANTED" as "WANTID," I would have appeared an illiterate fool, only confirming my copy editor's suspicions. As well as that, I was concerned that Independent gave off the wrong signal. Don't misunderstand me; you absolutely *should* be independent, but remember that I'm framing everything in the dating context for best results. Sadly, I think that Independent sounds a little too "fuck you!" to many men. You see, *men need to feel useful*. Humor us, for things haven't been the same since the invention of artificial insemination.

By Entertained, I mean *get a life*. Don't sulk about being single or become an HSM. Sure, being single isn't your end game, but it is a time of fun and freedom, a great adventure of discovering where life will take you next. Don't *nag* the Universe for a man; doing so only results in hastily choosing the wrong man. The Universe has this weird law that gives you what you want when you aren't stressed about it—like the proverbial couple who finally conceive a baby after they adopt a child.

Fill your schedule, create routines, join that class you've been meaning to join. These activities don't necessarily have to be sociable, but they give you an advantage. Joining a gym kills multiple birds with one stone. You get fit and toned, you are in a social environment, and you fill those blank spaces on your calendar. You have a life!

Commit to a night out with your friends once a week—yes, all engagements are difficult to get out of once you've committed to them. Being Entertained communicates to a man, "I'm not a needy loser waiting at home for a man, tapping my watch, and asking where he's been. I have my own life, thank you very much. But I will always make time for the *right* man—or better still, he could *join in* this life with me." This isn't being fake; it's how you should be anyway.

Life is for experiencing the thrill of opening new doors and being all you can be. The takeaway for Entertained is this:

You are available,
but you're happily single.

"D" Is for Dignified

To be "Dignified" means saying you are worthy of respect, and that starts with respecting yourself. For example, I'm not being old-fashioned when I say that sleeping with a man on a first date *purely to win his approval* is not dignified. (This book is titled *Kiss Fewer Frogs*, not *Fuck Fewer Frogs*.) If you're doing so for your own benefit, fair enough, but it's the Walk of Shame. Just keep a pair of flat shoes in the car. It's much less obvious when you aren't wearing heels.

Dignity is in short supply today. As you know, when supply goes down while demand remains constant, "prices" go up. Dignified is last on the WANTED list, but it should be first. *Up with male nonsense, you shall not put. If disrespected, you shall walk.* Yes, you're going to be that black-and-white unforgiving! You're welcome to crack open the door to him again, but he's on thin ice, and he will know it. *This is dating.* Marriage is a different matter.

Trust me, having the dignity to be brutally unforgiving of bullshit by simply walking away from it will only intrigue men and make them want you more (and the players will just move on). As long as you mean it, that's not playing games; it's a desirable side effect of having dignity. Every time you walk away from a situation or relationship you find disrespectful, you boost your love of self and send a clear message to men: "Take me seriously or else!"

Love of self comes before
love of another.

Putting your own standards higher than any man is player repellant. Plus, acknowledge the balance between wanting to please a man and not lowering your bar on what you consider respectful behavior. Be sure to align your respect requirements with your chosen prince's profile to be sure you aren't arguing against a person's nature. But in all cases, there is no excuse to disrespect yourself at the basic levels. Be discerning and carry yourself well.

Flicking back to something noted under "Assertive," I say imagine yourself as a VIP Lounge with a velvet rope around you wherever you go. The velvet rope conveys, "You can come inside if you are of a required standard and you know how to behave. Otherwise, I will take away the privilege." Remember, it's not barbed wire; it's velvet rope, and everyone wants to get behind it.

Again, this isn't playing games; Dignified reflects self-respect that you should have anyway. Prize yourself, and you shall be prized:

A man worth being with will do anything
to win the affections of a woman whose affections
are perceived as worth winning.

• • •

Punch this page to fist-bump me, for you are now a WANTED woman. Never settle. Be and stay WANTED—for yourself more than any man. Don't overthink it or get intimidated by this so-called "mystery of men;" WANTED could just as easily apply to men (simply invert the "W").

You've seen the Lies and the Revelations, you've chosen your prince, you've let the past go, and you are WANTED, so the door to love now opens wide to you. Just be careful who's holding that door for you.

part four

SYNCHRONIZE
WATCHES

Enter the Villains

"To know your enemy,
you must become your enemy."
- SUN TZU

Before you can reach your goal, you must deftly get around other players on the field in the way of your scoring. It's not personal; they have their goals just as you have yours. With *any* goal in life, people are usually in the way—the flakes, time wasters, and gatekeepers, as well as the intellectually challenged, ego trippers, and more. The trick is identifying them as quickly as possible and wasting the least amount of time with them.

To identify them is to *know* them.

As noted in Part One: *Kissing fewer frogs means applying an ultra-thick filter so you don't waste time with men who 1) aren't serious about finding a life partner at this time, and 2) are incompatible life partners for you.* This part focuses on the first point—a non-serious partner, which is a polite way of describing a "player" in the dating world.

What do we mean by "player"? Let's work with a more mature definition of our opponent than "asshole" (if for no other reason than to minimize your stress). Please, let's be adults about this definition:

♛

A player is someone whose relationship goals
are not aligned with yours at this time,
and who conceals that fact from you
in order to have sex with multiple women.

Okay, he's also an asshole.

Let's point the (middle) finger in the right direction, though. Some women conveniently yell "player!" simply because a guy didn't call her after a first date. Or because he dared to end the relationship. Or because he's trying hard by asking out multiple women. These hardly fit the bill.

Being a player includes an element of *willful deceit*, which can waste your time more than kissing a frog, especially if he's the prince profile you're looking for and you get caught in his web of lies.

Try not to get hot under the collar about players. Unless he has serious issues, no guy heads out for the night and says (in a British accent while twirling his mustache), "I really want to break a woman's heart tonight by sleeping with her and never calling her again, muhahaha-*haaaa!*" Sure, the typical single guy out for the night often *hopes* something happens; maybe he'll find a girl who'll sleep with him, kiss him (or maybe more), or give him her number. He might even be thinking about finding a girlfriend. The point is *he's not thinking the same way as you usually think when you head out for the night.* Although you're secretly wondering if you'll meet The One, he's not thinking that far ahead. And because women generally have an end game in mind (you'll see why later), it's tempting to assume men do as well. This all leads to assuming it was a guy's plan all along to sleep with her and never call her again, hence the bitter residue. This part of the book addresses the differences that *do* exist between males and females.

So, being a player often isn't malicious. And although knowing that doesn't solve your problem, realize that the Player Problem isn't as black and white as you may think. In fact, I venture to say that the person you aggressively call a "player" today could lovingly be called "hubby" tomorrow. This knowledge can also help you *forgive* past player experiences by not taking them personally and no longer giving them your energy.

Of course, having sex can be about as personal as it gets for you, but you'll shortly understand *how and why* men aren't always on the same page as women.

Let's categorize single men into three groups based on the traffic signal system: RED, YELLOW, and GREEN. Be aware that the same man can quickly change; being a red light today doesn't mean he can't be a green light tomorrow. Player or prince? That is the question.

CODE RED: "Player." This guy has absolutely zero intention of getting married or even into a serious relationship *at this time*. He may have just left an abusive relationship or marriage, or he may simply be young and needs to experiment. He carries contact details on several women, probably has a "booty-call black book," and may delight in seeing how many different women he can bed in any given time frame.

Of course, he likely knows you want what he doesn't, so he won't advertise his status. Instead, you have to spot the clues. However, if he's honest about wanting a "friend with benefits" or openly admits to "dating" (aka "tryouts") with various women who, like him, enter the arrangement with open eyes, then we can't put him in this category. Remember, being a player encompasses an element of *willful deception*. He could quickly change to CODE YELLOW if or when he calms down and sees the whole exercise as shallow, tough-going, or even hazardous. Typically, the older a man gets, the less likely he fits into this category. (I can personally vouch for that; even writing about this felt exhausting.)

CODE YELLOW: "Sleeping Prince." This is likely the largest group of single men, made up of the average single man going out for the night as described earlier: taking it as it comes, out for what he can get, but also suspecting that he will find a girlfriend from all the shenanigans and not being adverse to that idea. There is no ill intent; he just isn't thinking very far ahead. In the back of his mind, though, he also realizes that someday he will "settle down" (a less scary phrase for a guy than "marriage," so take note), and the older a man is in this group, the louder that "settle down" sound usually gets. This type can transition to CODE GREEN at any time.

CODE GREEN: "Prince." This man is actively seeking a partner, and he takes the dating scene seriously. He is not out to play the field.

So, obviously our work is with YELLOW and preferably GREEN status men, while keeping a watchful eye on RED status men (but not writing them off). Feel free to engage with RED status men (as you will, anyway, to assess their status). Stay in touch, but just don't sexually surrender until he changes status. He may fall for you as time goes on and turn GREEN (especially if you use the powers you'll learn about him). But don't let confirmation bias become a factor.

So, what other intel can you gather about CODE RED men? What drives them? Let's ask Hollywood.

Break the Bond

Stop munching popcorn and scan the audience inside a movie theater. You might notice men laughing at a time when their female partner doesn't appear amused at all. One such moment happens in the 2003 comedy movie *Old School*. As the groom stands at the altar awaiting his bride, his best man speaks to him secretly through whispering and cough-language: "Real smart, buddy, one vagina for the rest of your life!" and (coughing), "Don't do it . . . don't do it!" The male characters in *Old School* are portrayed as fugitives from unfaithful and/or oppressive women who are *trying to change them* (has Big Lie #2 sunk in yet?). This is a very popular film with men. Why?

Perhaps the question is best answered by Bond . . . James Bond. The James Bond franchise has endured with guys for more than sixty years, and the reason why has little to do with the cat-stroking villain taking two in the chest. The gadgets play a part, but many women also think gadgets are cool, and tons of other films feature technology. The success even has little to do with eye candy; those loose and leggy "Bond-girl" models can be found in many places in many media. Car chases and gunfights, yeah, we love 'em, but all action movies feature those—nothing special. So, what's the deal with 007?

It's the character himself, James Bond.

Mr. Bond doesn't commit to "one vagina for life" (well, he did once, but she was conveniently killed on the wedding night) or have to try hard to get women. They approach him and go to bed with him almost at the same moment. His skills in the bedroom are so legendary that he can turn a Soviet spy into a lovesick defector in one night.

Bond women are also portrayed as *expendable*; he's used them as human shields on more than one adventure. But, whatever, there are plenty more hoochies where she came from, and some of them had it coming for being deceitful.

Notice, though, how Bond women aren't exclusively portrayed as weak. They're also depicted as formidable power villains or capable sidekicks, right back to "Pussy Galore" in 1964's hit *Goldfinger*. Know this: *the message that resonates with men isn't necessarily that women are weak.* (This point is significant, as you will see shortly.)

Here's the key point: multigenerational male icon James Bond is a CODE RED player who *indiscriminately inseminates* a wide *variety* of women from *different nationalities and ethnicities*. James Bond is Licensed to *Fill*, and, as Carly Simon sang in *The Spy Who Loved Me*, "Nobody Does it Better."

You may gulp, but we're dealing with how the world *is*, not how we want it to be, because:

Rewards go to the realist.

This is a moment I warned you about when you nervously try to fact-check the details with male acquaintances. But they shake their heads and pretend "it's not true" while they squirm in their socks. Trust me, they're lying, even if they don't know it. This doesn't mean all men *do* or *should* act this way. Rather, I'm pinpointing the primal appeal of James Bond and how his stories affect his viewers. Underneath this apparent superficiality is a genuine deep love lying dormant for one special woman. But crossing the river of fire has to come first.

Obviously, not all men are players, so you need to know the opponent in order to avoid him. No man is born with the God-given purpose of jerking you around. When you see the profiles of the Seven Princes —the true *nature* each was born with—you'll see that none of them unanimously scream "player." So, it logically follows that a man *becomes* a player, usually *temporarily*, due to a combination of factors: nurture, prejudice, immaturity, circumstance, peer pressure, and so on. Therefore, since a man is not born as a player, it follows that within *all* men is the potential to *become* players in adulthood. (As horrifying as it sounds, you cannot deny the logic.) So, to explain the "player mind" is to explain the male mind—more specifically, the *darkest corner* of the male mind.

We can't blame Hollywood for this Player Problem. Movies might not always help the issue, but they're ultimately a business serving customers' requirements, so let's dig a little deeper. I'm about to take you down into the primal core of the human brain—a part that is essentially reptilian—so remove all sharp objects from your person.

Easy, Tiger

Both the male *and the female* mind is susceptible to primitive tendencies, sometimes in different ways. You need to be aware of these differences to avoid getting sidetracked by eye candy as well as by players.

Walk into a bookstore and ask the assistant for the section on "Finding a Wife." Good luck with that; your best chance might be under "Christian Books." Next, ask where you can find books on pickup lines, how to seduce a woman, how to give a woman five orgasms a night *et al.*, and you won't be as disappointed. Only about 10 percent of all books are purchased by men, and I'll bet a good portion of those have to do with getting laid (the rest being spy and war stories).

At first glance, you might despair. But in most cases, this dichotomy is actually women and men unconsciously pursuing the *same primal goal* in different ways. Men and women *aren't* from different planets; they're from different countries with different cultures and languages. Those differences exist because nature has conspired to create subtle changes in the programming of each sex, with both sexes unconsciously having the same goal: reproduction.

As explained in *The You Code:*

> *For over four billion years, an energy field of debated origin has vigorously fought for life to survive and thrive on this otherwise ordinary rock we call Earth, using a brilliantly intricate biological blueprint. This process occurred at a glacial pace, with The Energy Field having a primary goal*

of organisms reproducing. Each generation of reproduction gives The Energy Field the opportunity to select the choicest features from each of the mating organism's biological blueprint to create superior offspring, thus constantly improving and adapting each species for best chance of survival.

Imagine you're the Energy Field—call it Mother Nature—with that prime and entirely *selfish* goal of surviving and thriving on the planet, and you have these male and female animals to do that job with. How would *you* program each sex? *Be clinically and brutally honest!*

• • •

Mother Nature to Females:

Dear mama-to-be (well, duh, I need you to get knocked up),

You carry the egg, so you only have so many goes at this to help me make the human species better. Therefore, you can't just let any clown inseminate you. I need you to be selective, so only let the best genes pair with yours. Don't worry, I've programmed you to spot the best genes for *my* purposes.

By the way, in case you thought about disobeying me, I've added hormones to your body to make you feel broody, especially when you're ovulating. You don't need the guy to stick around, by the way. Just catch a rabbit or pick some berries—any pregnant woman or mother can do that—because I have other work for your sperm donor . . .

• • •

Mother Nature to Males:

Dear sperm donor,

Okay, buddy, give me all you've got. We need the best sperm to win here, and the only way of getting the best to choose from is to spread as much of it around as possible, in as many different varieties of female as possible. And may the best sperm win.

Genetic diversity is the secret of my success!

You have nothing to lose by complying. Knock yourself out; time is sperm, so get going. By the way, in case you thought about disobeying me, I've designed your reproductive plumbing so you'll get backed up—a bit like constipation—if you don't regularly ejaculate. It won't be nearly as satisfying if you DIY instead of in a vagina. Sorry, but all I care about is the human species evolving. Nothing personal.

Is that too much "real talk" for you? Don't shoot the messenger, and remember, I'm talking about the primitive side of us. I'm not excusing any bad behavior or saying that's how we *should* act. Take note of this programming, because the key difference between the sexes has a lot to answer for—including all the mystery about men. I hope you can sympathize with these primal afflictions.

One of the biggest complaints from married men with children is this: "She lost interest in me as soon as the kids came along." Maybe now you can see why this could be possible. Nature had its way with her, only *then* leaving her alone to have a "hooya!" moment.

Most important, you can now see what drives a player. And if there were a female equivalent of a player (acting as a deceitful and mind-less slave to nature's programming), perhaps it would involve get-ting pregnant accidentally on purpose. Only she would have a much greater consequence than a male, which makes her more selective.

♛

People of both sexes are capable of bad judgment
if they aren't mindful of their primitive programming.

I've personally known at least three men who, once all their children had left the nest, their wives suddenly got pregnant. "Yeah, I don't get it. All these years, the pill has been working fine, and now she suddenly got pregnant when the kids all left for college!" Hmmm, how odd . . .

Humans are animals. Humans were selected to rule the animal kingdom because of a fluke event that made apes stand on their hind legs. That allowed them to hunt better, which allowed their brains to grow and make us smarter than other animals. Most important, it gave us the *potential* for consciousness of thought and action (that is, the ability to stop carrying on like mindless *animals* as nature programmed us). When we are intoxicated, stressed, sick, or simply not mindful, those outer layers of the brain succumb to their animalistic core. This animalistic core is where the "players" live—for now.

Your Primal Programming

Have you noticed? Mother Nature is still living in our ancient past because she didn't get the memo about the most recent 1 percent of human existence being drastically different from our hunter-gatherer past. So, we are still programmed to be attracted to physical attributes that aren't as relevant as they once were. From *The You Code*:

> *At this purely superficial level, humans are unconsciously scanning for facial symmetry in a potential partner because this indicates healthy genes. Fair hair on a female suggests higher estrogen levels, meaning higher fertility. Heterosexual males are unconsciously assessing a female's hip-to-waist ratio for the ideal of 10:8 for the purposes of healthy impregnation and birthing, and mammary glands for milk production . . . Heterosexual females are unconsciously assessing for small and muscular buttocks for sexual thrusting and deep insemination, and yes, penis length, for ejaculation as close to the awaiting egg as possible. Superficial attraction is a healthy and normal thing that The Energy Field has ingeniously and insidiously installed in our hardwiring . . .*

> *. . . In this sense, The Energy Field's agenda is not aligned with your personal happiness or even your sexual pleasure. For example, on the popular topic of penis size (or unpopular, depending on one's penis size), heterosexual females who act mindlessly are genetically programmed to be attracted to longer penises, perhaps even creating a self-fulfilling prophecy, and yet female orgasm induces from two points*

*totally unrelated to penis length. There is no sexual bliss for
a female in a large object banging against her cervix, but it
creates juicy urban myths and mindless chatter.*

So, you see, you can get sidetracked by the wrong things if you're
not mindful of your basic programming. We think we're being
all high-tech when we swipe a human being's face to the left on a
dating app, but we're actually behaving in a highly primitive way.
Mother Nature couldn't give a damn about your sexual joy or your
love affair with your chosen prince or the God-given purpose of
your Genetype. (Note: six out of the seven purposes of the female
Genetypes have nothing to do with childbirth.) Mother Nature just
wants you to obey her programming.

Let's examine other ways this primal programming influences us
and maybe explain what could have happened to you, given that:

A player is a man who doesn't want commitment but,
like all men, still has a NEED for sex.

So, if you've ever been abandoned after having sex, don't think it is
anything to do with your body or sexual technique. Find forgiveness
so you can leave that hurt in the past. How? By understanding what's
going on with certain mindless men. Ninety-nine percent of sexually
healthy men masturbate (and the other 1 percent are liars). So, don't
think male masturbation is "disgusting"; it's different for males in
that if they don't regularly release the *pressure* down below, a gasket
will blow.

Men can't focus without having sex, which gives them two choices —one partner or several—and you only want the man who chooses correctly. But if you were thinking of charitably helping a brother out with his release problem, don't forget D for Dignified. Having sex too soon means he won't respect you, which means he won't call you again, which means he becomes a player that, in a way, *you both created.*

Primal programming also explains why most men are so repulsed by a woman trying to change him (Big Lie #2). It also explains the famous male pride you're so scared to prick:

♛

To the primitive male brain,
being told that he needs to change
equates to telling him he (his seed)
is inadequate.

"Inadequate" is a *killer* word for men, and now you know why. You also know why Viagra was one of the fastest-selling drugs in history. If you want to insult a man where it hurts most (please don't, though), make it about *inadequacy.* Conversely, if you want to make a man feel good, make it about *adequacy.* Saying you want to change him is like trying to destroy him, and that may sound silly to you, but now you can see how each of you is programmed differently. This "male pride" gets famously mistaken for male ego when it's actually more about nature than nurture. (Note: ego is a function of nurture.) If you want to lose a guy, keep trying to change him, which translates to "She thinks I'm inadequate.

Perhaps another woman will think I *am* adequate." This is why, as I mentioned under E for Entertained, *a man needs to feel useful.* This is also why super-adequate James Bond has sex with women who are often portrayed as strong, not weak. It's a great compliment that a strong (WANTED) woman would want a man's seed; it makes him feel *adequate.*

Perhaps you can also understand why being with a virgin is a turn-on for a man, although not so much for a woman. Obviously, inseminating a virgin means virtually guaranteed success of his genes being passed on if she gets pregnant because he's the first one to attempt it with her, whereas to a woman it makes no difference how many women the man has previously had sex with. This leads me to introduce into the contemporary dating context something called The Virgin Delusion—what I was getting at in N for Naughty when saying you need to sound more sex-*curious* than sex-*experienced.*

Look, you know you're not a virgin, and he knows you're not a virgin, but people believe what they want to believe. Don't lie; just be economical with the truth, and let his imagination fill in the blanks. Less is more, so feed the Virgin Delusion.

"Mysteries" about Men

Next, let's address common "mysteries" about men that women have—ones you should now be able to answer for yourself (even though you won't like those answers):

Common Question 1: "Why, after he left me, does he say he still loves me?"

> *Answer: Because he still wants to have sex with you and block you from meeting other men (competing sperm). If he truly loved you, he would've stayed with you, or he would return and commit to you properly.*

Common Question 2: "Why, after cheating, do men often say the woman he had sex with meant nothing to him?"

> *Answer: Because the woman he had sex with meant nothing to him.*

Get it? Overthinking about men gives them too much credit. In both of those questions, the man involved literally behaved like an *animal*; he had yet to transcend to *human being* in the romantic sense. If my evil plan has worked, you will think more carefully before allowing a man anywhere near your sacred center, which also creates the desirable side effect of placing the velvet rope around you. If a player's goalpost is solely having sex, then removing the goalpost until you feel comfortable with him is like playing the ultimate defense in the dating game.

If a woman's ace card is sex,
and a man's is commitment,
too many women play their ace card
way too early.

Until a man's watch is no longer set to Primal Time, *and until he truly sees you as a human being with feelings instead of an animal insemination target*, consider him a player risk. So, if you want to kiss fewer frogs, do your best to eliminate the player risk.

Get Prepared with Playdar

Now that you know what you're dealing with, let's set you up with Player Radar or "Playdar." Too many red flags mean the player risk goes up, but to keep the balance, don't turn into a Man-hating Ice Queen (MIQ). Knowing what drives players is a powerful filter. That's why you want to be somewhere in the middle of the spectrum between HSM (Husband-Seeking Missile) and MIQ (Man-hating Ice Queen).

Given the confusion about what the "rules" are, both CODE RED and CODE YELLOW guys can take advantage of the blurry boundaries in the dating world. "Dating" is open to interpretation. Most people assume that means it's okay to go on "dates" with different people, but what exactly is "allowed" to happen on these "dates"? Some see it as a license to sleep around and act like a player, but many women wouldn't do certain things if they knew a guy was also seeing other women. That requires creating your own set of "rules" and repainting your boundary lines. Here are a few suggestions for doing that:

1. Be direct. Most men appreciate direct language. (Indirect language is one of their biggest complaints.) If you need clarification on where you stand, politely ask your question at a suitable moment, perhaps as he makes further advances. For example, "Are we exclusive to each other now?" Until you're exclusive, you know not to take things beyond a certain level, emotionally and/or sexually. Of course, this doesn't mean he will be truthful, so ask the question to his face, *not* by text, and carefully watch how he responds. *Trust your heart, not your (prejudiced) head!*

2. "All is fair" when it comes to first dates. It's okay to be going on first, even second dates, with multiple people—that's what dating is: "tryouts" for suitability. This might involve kissing and touching but not having sex. If you're the seventh first date for the same guy in the same week, then strictly speaking, he's not really a player. Arguably, he's an over-enthusiastic CODE GREEN. Same rule goes for you, so use it.

3. If and when you both agree you're exclusive to one another (and you're convinced he's being truthful), you've crossed a line regarding acceptable and unacceptable behavior, a kind of unspoken verbal agreement. Most men appreciate clearly marked boundaries. (If you have young sons, you'll know this. Boys tend to misbehave more frequently without having a set of cause-and-effect rules to follow.) If the guy in question had dishonorable intentions, you've sent him a clear message that to sleep with you and then dump you would make him an even more dishonorable dirtbag than before. Remember, players aren't born evil. They're still human beings, and this "exclusive boundary" can make players walk away while princes step forward. They will appreciate your Assertiveness, Tastefulness, and Dignified-ness, even your Entertained-ness, so a lot of boxes get ticked in one useful move. If, after agreeing to be exclusive with you, you discover he's still dating, then you have an unequivocal breach of trust, and the D for Dignified action plan kicks in. Otherwise, let your gut guide you about what happens next and when, giving the guy the full benefit of the doubt and staying WANTED. *By the way, being exclusive covers both of you!*

4. Remember, eye-candy, primal attraction, and feelings for someone can interfere with your Playdar, so stay objective! Here are a few more tips to do that:

- At first contact or on the first date, listen for language that's out of place for most guys but is common among women. For example, asking about your star sign is a flag that he's possibly read something on how to "get" women. It could be innocent, of course, but probe deeper and see how much he really knows about what he's just said. I've never met a guy who was into astrology (although some must exist), but it's not common. It's like a guy asking you to name your favorite character in the TV series *Sex and the City*. Guys generally don't watch shows like that! Another flagged conversation would be to use too much classic "girl bait," like fairy-tale language. None of these flags means he's a player necessarily; it merely means you've got a ping on your Playdar that needs to be monitored. Don't become overly defensive or you'll give off the wrong energy.

- Under W for Womanly, I explained how, at a man and woman's first encounter, the man typically doesn't move past visuals, but a woman generally will—automatically. Now, this should make sense; all the while he's on Primal Time, he unconsciously sees you as an insemination target. You also are still unconsciously on Primal Time, but you've moved on to "other considerations" because you are naturally more selective. Use this moment wisely to ask indirect questions I'll show you in Part Six while he is distracted by W for Womanly.

- Mother Nature may have conspired against the sexes to suit her own agenda, but part of the deal was giving animals a sixth sense for their survival. Humans have complacently sat at the top of the food chain for so long that we've either shut off our sixth sense or forgotten how to use it. Learn to trust your gut again (not your head!), and know that if something *feels* off, it probably is.

Primal Time Viewing

Before you allow a serious relationship to proceed to the ultimate level of intimacy, both of you should be off Primal Time and have your watches synchronized for experiences beyond Mother Nature's basic programming.

Love is the rickety rope bridge that carries us across the abyss from animal to human being. Ancient rites of passage performed by shamans had animals present to symbolize this distinction between humans and mindless animals. (We see the legacy of this every Christmas in the nativity. Can you imagine a nativity without animals?) Folk-tale and fairy-tale villains like the Big Bad Wolf are there to caution us about slipping back into our animalistic ways. They're also metaphors for what's "out there" if we aren't mindful. The story of *Beauty and the Beast* has been traced back over four thousand years as a tale of how kindness and love overcome the half-animal man—qualities that return him to humanity. Like fairy tales, our most enduring stories have these common threads: the conflict of light and darkness, and how love and compassion win the day.

But just as it's within all men to behave *badly*, it's also within them to behave *well*, and ultimately, most men *do* make the right choice, as the answer to this next common question illustrates:

Common Question 3: "Why, after a guy leaves a long-term relationship because of commitment issues, does he often end up quickly marrying the first girl he meets?"

> *Answer: Because the James Bond/playboy fantasy called him away. Then, when the harsh, contrasting reality of an empty single life and losing what he had hits home, he rushes back to the path he previously ran away from—the bittersweet path of love.*

• • •

Every good story has villains because deep down we know that the reward tastes all the sweeter for adversity. Your story is no different. Well done for making it through the darkest part of our journey, for it's always darkest before the dawn. Now, let's go find your prince.

part five

FISH
IN A
BARREL

Be Careful What You Fish For

Life can dramatically change in a single *second*.

The next task is to expose you to as many of those potentially life-changing seconds as possible. You now need to get in front of as many of your chosen "prince-clones" as possible, in the fastest time possible, with the least amount of effort. You're playing a numbers game here, plain and simple, and this is a pivotal step in fast tracking your fairy tale ending.

What's the secret to finding your chosen prince? *Focus*.

The other night, a completely sober man accidentally drove his car into my front yard. He got out, handed me a piece of my fence, and said, "I was looking for Walmart." I replied, "Well, it's not in my front yard. And the nearest Walmart is over thirty minutes away from here." Don't be like that poor unfortunate soul. Race car drivers are taught that if you find yourself skidding off the track toward the wall, they're tempted to look at the wall, but they must fight that reaction and instead look back at the track. That's where you want to be. Life is like that, because . . .

What you focus on is what you get.

The Law of Attraction states that *you can get whatever you focus on*, and it's true. But this law is often misunderstood and incorrectly used. Many people attempt to focus on such nebulous things as money or marriage or health, and then they wonder why they don't materialize any of them. In a similar vein, people *blame* the Law of Attraction for all the bad stuff that happens to them: "What the . . . ! I never focused on getting food poisoning!"

The key to using the Law of Attraction is *specificity*—that is, being highly specific about *what* you want and *when* you want it by. Use the Law of Attraction correctly, and you only need to understand one thing: *be careful what you wish for, because it's going to happen.*

Calibrate your senses to what you desire. Let's say you woke up today with a burning desire to own a Toyota Camry automobile. (The make and model aren't important; this is just an example. When I do this exercise in seminars, you'd be amazed how many people get stuck on the type of car I chose. That's ironic, considering this is an exercise on focus!)

Then, as you drive to work, you notice more Toyota Camrys on the road than you saw yesterday, right? How can this be? The number of that vehicle type did not magically increase overnight; it's that today, you are *noticing* them. This phenomenon occurred because your senses were suddenly calibrated to notice Camrys.

♛

Calibrate your senses to notice
your chosen prince profile, and let the
Law of Attraction start working for you.

You already possess the crucial specificity you need to make the Law of Attraction work, because you have a specific type of person in mind. Now is the time to apply this knowledge in the real world. First, *know the Genetype profile of your chosen prince like the back of your hand*—let him become your "Toyota Camry." And remember, you only need to find *one* out of the millions of his clones out there.

Yes, be careful what you fish for; there are plenty of fish under the sea. But you will start to *notice* and close in on only one kind of fish—the "fish" (a prince Genetype) you have come to know well. Even at this initial stage, you *can* and *will* begin making your chosen prince a part of your world.

Let's step out of the classroom and transform this book into a handbook with bulleted action steps. It also has breakout sections for each of the Seven Princes.

Here is where you'll start seeing what you've read so far come together!

Don't worry about the competition; your competitors are too preoccupied with wishing, waiting, and whining to be a threat. Do you want to join their whining ranks or not? If not, go full speed ahead!

Before you get going, though, please appreciate that *there will be effort involved.* Half-assed efforts get and deserve half-assed results. When it comes to *anything* you want in life, the difference between the people who get what they want and those who don't—the winners versus losers—is because winners are prepared to do what losers are not.

The people who get what they want
become A for Assertive, and they are not deterred
by previous failures.

Going forward, you'll see a division into "online" and "offline" followed by customized comments for each prince. Do you recall this formula? *Compatibility + Chemistry = Life Partner.* That's still in play in the breakout sessions that follow.

Online is a good way to check for compatibility first.
Offline is a good way to check for chemistry first.

Fortunately, you don't need to choose between online or offline. Given that each has its own set of advantages, you can and should employ both. Be sure to use the right tool for the right job, knowing that all roads lead to the off-line world.

First, let's go online.

Casting a Wide Net—Online

I have to assume you're starting from zero, so if anything seems obvious to you, treat it as a new way of looking at the issue. There's a bit of setup work here, but it's like starting a business—a one-time deal that you will continually benefit from.

Benefits of Online Dating

- A reminder of the benefits of online dating, especially with your new and unique advantage in mind:

- Online dating gives you the ability to fish where the fish are. It has, in theory, given you access to an ocean full of fish who are single and looking for a partner. This can't be achieved by walking into a bar where numbers are limited. That approach is "hit or miss" on any given night, and you don't know who, if anyone, might be single.

- Online dating sites allow you to customize the "bait" for your chosen prince, a discussion we will come to. Be sure the dating site you're using doesn't try to matchmake for you (another example of technology making life harder); you need the ability to choose for yourself, specifically to be able to write the specs "What I'm looking for in a partner" and "About me."

- Online dating gives you the ability to check if your "Are we exclusive now?" agreement has been broken. You can simply see if and when a guy was last on the dating site. Yes, most guys really are that dumb.

The Optimal User Profile—Photos

- I don't know why a debate exists about using photos or not when you understand how males think (or don't think). Men are visual, and, at this point in the proceedings (like it or not), they are on Primal Time. Stand out or step off! You have a fraction of a second to snag a man's fast-scanning eye.

Remember, it's a numbers game, so play it. Previously in this book, you learned what that primal eye is scanning for. That's why you should post good-quality photos with you looking your best. Ideally, your photos are studio shots with professional makeup and hair so you can appear as good as if it were your wedding day. There is nothing deceptive about this. It's still you. And if/when you meet, he has the opportunity to transition from Primal Time to something of deeper quality, based on your high-quality photo. *Au naturel* photos may sound noble, but during their initial scans, most men aren't able or willing to see beyond visuals. However, don't be tempted to use photos of you from twenty years ago—no older than a few years ago, please.

• Photos are a good way to *show*, not *tell* that you are WANTED, that you are particularly Womanly, Tasteful, Entertained, even Dignified if you exude a certain demeanor.

• Don't let your photos be "weird." You may think it's cute or funny to superimpose animal features on your face and/or blow up the size of your eyes. Your chosen prince might even think it's cute. But your enemy is the fast-scanning primal male eye, and he wants to see what's under all the nonsense. Plus, let's hope he isn't into dating animals.

• You with a BFF in the photo? Yes, I've seen this a lot. But then the guy wonders which one is the woman who is dating, or, in his wildest fantasies, he hopes he gets two for the price of one. In any case, it doesn't matter how great your BFF is; "two" is not the desired effect you want. *Note*: Animals and children in the profile photo are also a distraction for the primal male eye.

- You'd think it would be a given that you don't look suicidal in your photo, *but you would not believe how many women's photos actually look like that!* You don't have to beam out a smile that pales the sunlight, but just don't look sad. Why would any man want to date a woman who looks like she lost her only friend?

- Given that sexual variety triggers the primal male brain, he is programmed to foster genetic diversity, which aligns with your photo gallery. Consider a *variety* of looks, poses, hair-styles, outfits, and more. Ensure your best, clearest headshot is the one on display for your profile.

- No overly sexual photos, please. Revealing too much or posting slutty poses tells a guy you're either a pro or an easy sex target.

The Optimal User Profile—Copywriting 101 (the written section)

- I cannot overemphasize this enough: *Make the copy all about him, not you.* This is a basic selling technique, and yes, you are selling yourself. Even in the "About me" section, gear the wording toward him as much as possible. For example (slyly by a woman who is targeting physically driven Prince 6), you write: "I'm a fitness fanatic, and I hope you are too." Notice how the woman in that example is writing her profile as if she's actually speaking to the one person reading—yes, one person—since only one person reads at any given time. Don't write: "Hey, all you guys out there, let me tell you all about sexy me, blah, blah, blah." Remember, there is only one reader you care about, and he only cares about himself (at this point in time). YOU language is how your words can leap off the screen and hit him between the eyes. The first lesson I teach rookie copywriters is this simple one: *the most powerful word in the English language is "YOU." Use it!*

• Although your photo is the first thing he will look at, a headline written under it is a close second. Needless to say, most headlines completely blow, so take this time and opportunity to stand out. "hi" is not a headline (note the lower case "h," which means the person is too lazy to even hold down the caps lock key, *plus* "hi" translates to being perceived as an unenthusiastic, hard-work date). Yet "hi" is perhaps the most commonly used "headline" on dating sites. Don't be lame. A headline's purpose is to attract and hold someone's attention in a way that meets that person's desires. It's a punchy way to tie in a relevant aspect of yourself with your chosen prince's Dominant Driver. For example, Prince 5 is driven by a need for freedom, so an appealing headline for him (perhaps written by a woman who is spiritual and sensitive to energy) might say: "Let's be free, together" or "Faithful and Free. Are you?" (Notice how I was careful to ensure "freedom" wasn't misinterpreted as promiscuity. Feed the Virgin Delusion; don't starve it.) Now, you don't need to call a creative brainstorming meeting or hire an ad agency. It's not rocket science. Simply walk in *his* shoes, not yours. Know your target audience intimately, and the right headline will come naturally. (In the breakout session, you'll find suggested headline hooks for each prince. Make them your own.)

• Make your sentences short, punchy, and straight to the point. Men appreciate direct language.

- No ranting about past exes or men in general (= damaged goods and/or MIQ). No long-winded autobiographies (= boring date, conceited wife). No fussy list of requirements (= high maintenance). Make it all about *him*. After all, people are generally self-focused. Anything you say about yourself should be somehow positioned to "make it," so it actually feels like it's about *him*. And, of course, make sure you're ticking as many of the WANTED boxes as possible.

- Show, don't tell. For example, instead of saying, "I'm a very compassionate person," say, "In my spare time, I do charity work." Sharing details about your contributions sounds more credible and powerful than making a statement.

- When completing your online user profile, you're not lying, you're simply taking the points about you that are most appealing to your prince's profile. It's like when a good realtor shows someone a house; if the potential buyer has children, the realtor might point out the location of good schools and nearby playgrounds. If your chosen guy is Prince 1 (a person who likes to bring order from chaos), and you happen to be a very tidy person, then you would state details you may not have considered before you were aware of Genetypes. But if you're having to stop being yourself to fit this prince, you may reconsider your choice. *The prince you choose isn't set in stone.* As your real-world experiences unfold, I encourage you to challenge your choice, so you can be as certain as possible.

- If your profile has a "Dislikes" section, you have an opportunity to name dislikes that you and your chosen prince share to create an immediate connection, but don't make them too negative or abusive. Spin everything in a positive way. For example, if targeting Prince 3 (a person who likes to bring chaos from order), you might say a dislike of yours is "Doing the same thing every day," but then you could add, "but that's what evenings and weekends are for, right?!"

- Phrase what you say in terms of features and benefits. For example, saying "I love to cook!" is great as a feature for *you*, but take it further so it also becomes a benefit for *him*. You would say, "I love to cook, so I hope you like good food!" Tick for the A and E boxes, also. Betting that a guy likes good food was hardly risky. She didn't specify what type of food she likes to cook in case the guy reading hated that type. So, she let his imagination fill in the blanks by using another copywriting secret: *the power of suggestion*. She also writes as if it's a "done deal" that the person reading wants her (the unspoken sentence: well, duh, you'd be a fool not to want me!), also known as "the assumptive close." Note how she also said, "So, I hope YOU like good food." The man reading feels like the only man in the world, suggesting that's how she will make him feel. Wow, all that from one simple and perfectly "innocent" sentence.

Next is offline, aka the real world.

Where the People Are—Offline

When it comes to finding your prince in the off-line world, the process obviously isn't nearly as scientific, but it *is* a far better way to quickly have a filter for chemistry, which can quickly lead to a filter for compatibility when you intimately know your chosen prince's profile (more on this in Part Six). But, here's the funny thing about the real world:

At first contact, any possible chemistry match
could be compromised
by the energy each person gives off.

When we are having a bad day, we can give off negative energy, or if we are feeling insecure and lack confidence, people can sense it. This means two things: 1) you can't write people off purely because the chemistry seems off, and 2) *your* energy on any given day can attract or repel suitable males. You can't control his energy, but you can control yours. This is another reason for Part Three on the WANTED concept—to help ensure your energy isn't getting between you and any possible chemistry match in the real world.

So, to maximize opportunity where real people are, remember this:

Your day will go the same way
as the corners of your mouth.

If you feel a bad day coming on, break the downward spiral with a positive act like this: Go to a drive-through for comfort food to make you feel better. Place your order, and then when you pay your bill, ask how much the driver of the car behind you needs to pay. If it's a reasonable amount, tell the cashier you'll pay for it. It could just be a coffee at Starbucks. Don't ask for thanks from the cashier or the person behind you; just pay and drive away. For all you know, that inexpensive act of kindness could be the difference between someone ending it all or carrying on, and that truly changes the world. This is compassion and music to your soul. *Doing this becomes your happiness reset button, allowing you to begin again.*

With your positive energy in gear, you can enjoy the benefits of finding your prince in the off-line world. Here are some pointers and ideas:

- Turn on your "Toyota Camry" radar mentioned earlier.

- Get especially familiar with only one of the prince profiles. Become an expert in your chosen prince-clone. The more practice you can get at quickly identifying him, the better. I speak from experience when I say that, after enough practice, you will know a person's Genetype within a few minutes of first contact—sometimes without saying a word (depending on the type). FYI, the breakout session to follow highlights some fast identification clues for each of the types.

- There is no one magical place where all the single guys hang out. Yes, I get asked this a lot. Single guys, like every other human being, wander around doing their thing—working, grocery shopping, socializing, and so on. Take single men down from the pedestal and go about your normal business. Be prepared to bump into him—without being self-conscious if you're wearing sweatpants on a bad hair day. (In the breakout session are listed common locations for each of the princes, but realistically, they are everywhere.)

• The more sociable you can make yourself, the better. Talk to anyone and everyone; don't be shy or aloof. You never know where events will take you, even if not romantically. Take a moment to examine your life and consider how many great paths opened to you because you allowed yourself to engage with someone. Always accept invitations to events; just go. You can always have a friend call you with a pretend "emergency" if you need to escape. Again, it's a numbers game. Also, this is ticking your E for Entertained box, so you're killing two birds with one stone.

• Enjoy a "Hooya!" moment by getting out of your own little world with its own little problems and master the art of eavesdropping. Look at "hovering and listening" as a great, risk-free way to notice things that could signal your prince's profile.

• If being sociable is a struggle for you, then train yourself as you would by going to the gym. For many functions, the brain muscle needs building through the simple processes of habit and positive feedback loops. Give yourself a goal of initiating between five and ten conversations with an unknown male each week. Make sure you're in a public place that provides a safe environment for sharing (and other safety factors). For example, if you're sitting at a bar or waiting in a line about to order food (ideally after careful eavesdropping), ask a guy, "Is there anything you'd recommend?" or "Wow, that looks good. What did you order?" That everyday act between two humans counts toward your target of five to ten conversations a week. You've opened the door to further exchanges between the two of you, so don't simply run off after he answers. And be sure your comment isn't a negative one like, "Geez, what's taking them so long?"

- Be on the lookout for singles nights mixers, including speed-dating events. Once you're an expert on your prince's profile, speed dating suddenly takes on a whole new level of usefulness!

- To help with "Entertained," join an evening class with a topic that's not predominantly female. Many men have gotten wise to this tactic with single women, so don't choose one like car mechanics that obviously makes you outnumbered by men. Taking evening classes is also an excellent way to employ prince-profiling because they're targeted to interests and hobbies. (More about this in the breakout session.) Also, joining a gym or any sports club ticks several boxes at once, so choose one that is as much about a social scene as an athletic endeavor.

- Choose three good restaurants where you can eat at the bar and integrate as one of the "regulars." Get to know the staff on first-name terms—everyone from the valet parkers to the bartenders. Tip them well! They can offer a great focal point of who is who, and who is single. And they can be great introducers! Be sure to always order the same drink so the bartender can have it ready for you without asking. This sends a message to other patrons that you're "cool" and some- one worth knowing. Meet and speak to the other regulars— not just other singles, but couples, too. In fact, speaking to couples has gotten me many date referrals, and it should do for you too. "Oh my God, Gary, we have got to introduce her to Jack! He would love her, right?" Of course, ask questions about "Jack" to assess his Genetype. If he's a match, planning a subsequent dinner as a foursome is safe and low pressure.

- Identifying *your* prince from other princes becomes easier when you think of it as a process of deduction. You have only seven possibilities, and you can quickly eliminate half of those within minutes.

- *Important note*: It's not a given that your chosen prince for *compatibility* will be a *chemistry* match. In fact, once you've found the desired prince profile, you can expect to be disappointed about the chemistry half of the time (a rough guess). This does not necessarily mean you chose the wrong prince.

Okay, let's next talk specifics on how to find your man with the Seven Princes breakout session. Here's where the magic begins, especially online. When you create or re-create your user profile on the dating site, you can customize it according to your chosen prince's likely requirements.

Catch of the Day

> *"Personally, I am very fond of strawberries and cream,*
> *but I have found that for some strange reason, fish prefer worms.*
> *So, when I went fishing, I didn't think about what I wanted.*
> *I thought about what they wanted. I didn't bait the hook with*
> *strawberries and cream. Rather, I dangled a worm or grasshopper*
> *in front of the fish and said: 'Wouldn't you like to have that?'"*
> – DALE CARNEGIE, How to Win Friends and Influence People

After studying, coaching, and interacting with the fourteen male and female Genetypes for over a decade, this observation never ceases to astound me: *how incredibly different the Genetypes are from each other*. It's because what drives them at their core—their unconscious priorities in life or Dominant Drivers—aren't the same.

Each Genetype generally views the world through its own Genetypal lens—a factor that can sow disharmony among people. Generally, we are ignorant about the existence of these Genetypes, so we work against each other instead of balancing each other as a good team does. It seems like each Genetype has its own language, and, just as people travel in a foreign land dealing with a foreign language, they feel relief and joy when they find someone who understands what they are saying.

> This "language" is the language of each person's
> soul. Therefore, you must become fluent in the
> language of your chosen prince to both win him
> and keep him—as no other woman ever could.

Breakout Session Notes

- Please appreciate that I can only offer probabilities when it comes to finding and identifying a Genetype. This breakout session offers possible jobs each prince is likely to be doing, social locations most frequented, probable dress code, commonplace visual cues, etc. Warning: *No single box that's ticked here is enough to assume anything.* Any prince can be anywhere, acting in any way, at any time, dressed in any way. However, the more boxes that get ticked, the more likely you've found him. Of course, the best way to know is to engage him, and that's what Part Six addresses.

• Online, when completing the important "About me" and "What I'm looking for in a man" sections, write using your own words. Even the dumbest guys might start to smell a fake by seeing the same paragraph all over women's dating profiles.

• You will find bullet points in each of the user profile sections. Remember, you are attempting to speak the language of his soul. Therefore, write with a photocopy of his profile (from Part Two of this book) next to you. Don't get intimidated about writing. Everyone can write! Forget the voice of your grade-school English teacher and simply write as you would speak. Begin each "What I'm looking for" section with "You're a man who . . ." and let it flow.

• Because all of the suggested bullets may not apply, tap into the aspects about yourself that fit best.

Finding Prince 1

Online

Additional photo tips:

- Ensure one shot looks as if you're accompanying him to a corporate event, and, if applicable, one of you at work if in a management setting.
- Clothing and appearance should be on the conservative side.

Headline hooks:

- Reliability, dependability, stability
- Partners in life and career
- "Wing woman"
- Career, professional language

"About me" ideas:

- I'm organized, clean, and tidy.
- I am supportive of my man's career and help him climb the ladder.
- I'm a team player, and it's okay for us both to have a career.
- I love to help solve problems and resolve differences—I'm inspiring.

"What I'm looking for in a man" ideas:

- Career-focused
- Reliable

- Logical
- Rules follower
- Likes to take charge

"Dislikes" ideas:

- Being dramatic (doesn't understand why women can be so illogical and overly emotional)
- Being disorganized, creating chaos
- Lacking structure and routine
- Having no ambition in life

Offline

Probable jobs found in:

- Highly varied, mostly corporate and professional settings
- Vocations involving technology and rules
- Doctor, lawyer, accountant, management, networks, banking

Possible evening classes found at:

- Educational or vocational school (to further career)
- Mandarin language (for business with China)

Visual clues:

- Unassuming, showing a pragmatic demeanor
- Blending in, not ostentatious or loud
- Dressing conservatively
- Carrying a laptop or tablet, business cards at the ready, perhaps two cell phones

Eavesdropping notes:

- Work, work, work
- Schmoozing language, diplomatic, polite but forced chuckles
- Using "MBA-speak" and industry jargon
- Showing little variance in tone—emotionless, calculated, political

Good ice breakers:

- Requesting professional advice or anything pertaining to his profession
- Asking who is hiring for management or professionals in the area
- Offering tips for networking, recruitment, useful business apps, etc. (perhaps triggered by a problem he was discussing)

Places commonly found:

- Golf course/club
- Professional locations such as offices
- Happy hour in or close to business centers
- Popular business lunch spots (those guaranteeing quick service)

Finding Prince 2

Online

Additional photo tips:

- Enjoying a quiet life at home
- Reading a book
- Traveling
- Not looking too dressed up

Headline hooks:

- Life partner who needs space
- Home is our castle
- The intelligent choice

"About me" ideas:

- I need space without any catches or insecurities, but "I am faithful."
- I love staying indoors, but also love to travel and enjoy new experiences.
- I enjoy deep conversations and don't need to be all that sociable.
- I have multiple interests.

"What I'm looking for in a man" ideas:

- Learned, loves to read
- Eclectic range of interests, multilayered
- Also wants space and alone time
- Can engage in deep, theoretical conversations with me

"Dislikes" ideas:

- Mindless masses, conventional thinking
- Lack of privacy
- People being fools or fake

Offline

Probable jobs found in:

- Teaching, information centers, government
- Working from home

Possible evening classes found at:

- Anything/anywhere that adds to his intellect
- Musical instruments, languages
- Further education

Visual clues:

- Unfashionable but practical clothing
- Introverted, aloof
- Latent tension when away from home
- Hyperfocused

Eavesdropping notes:

- Enjoying silence
- Allowing enthusiasm or rants to burst out of nowhere

- Teaching others, learning, engaging in deep conversation
- Not feeling comfortable in public but can quickly jump into a stimulating conversation

Good ice breakers:

- Inquiring about book recommendations and book he has in his hand
- Commenting on mutually witnessed herd behavior
- Discussing unusual travel destinations of mutual interest

Places commonly found:

- At home
- Libraries, bookstores
- Schools and colleges

Finding Prince 3

Online

Additional photo tips:

- Variety, different settings and styles
- Appreciating art; a gallery, library, theater, concert, etc.
- Fashionable and feminine

Headline hooks:

- Paired by passion
- Your muse, free spirit
- Build a fire, create a future together

"About me" ideas:

- I'm passionate—"Complacency kills one's spirit."
- I'm romantic—"I kiss like I mean it."
- I love doing new things.
- I hate bullshit and love the truth.
- I love working on or helping with creative projects.

"What I'm looking for in a man" ideas:

- Spontaneous, passionate, romantic
- Speaks his mind (good or bad), honest, no BS
- Creative and focused on projects
- Wants the world to wake up

"Dislikes" ideas:

- Monotony and routine, contrived situations
- Attending schmoozy events
- People being fake
- Conformity, everyone thinking the same way
- The Establishment, the sheep
- Not being "rock and roll" about things

Offline

Probable jobs found in:

- Creative arts of any kind, including writers, musicians, chefs, sculptors, film directors
- Architecture, graphic design, advertising (creative department)

Possible evening classes found at:

- Music lessons
- Cooking, wine tasting
- Writing groups

Visual clues:

- Speaking with hands (like Italian stereotype), flamboyant
- Wearing loose, comfortable clothing, casual but fashionable if outside the home. (Inside the home anything goes, and it's often bizarre.)

- Showing intense eyes and expressions that could be mistaken for sadness, aloofness, or introversion
- Appearing to be searching, daydreaming, with mental cogs turning

Eavesdropping notes:

- Strangers initiate conversations with him (like moths to the flame)
- Shows passionate enthusiasm or throws a tantrum, often in the same few minutes
- Overreacts, participates in heated discussions
- Enjoys creative projects, deadlines, patrons, gigs
- Says what most people think but dare not say aloud

Good ice breakers:

- If possible, praise his work—this is huge.
- Provide input on a creative discussion overheard. "Cool, what if . . ."
- Comment on mutually witnessed herd mentality.

Places commonly found:

- Wherever the "studio" is—the birthplace of his creation
- Drinking establishments, chic restaurants that turn food into art
- Bookstores, galleries, theaters, etc.
- Home

Finding Prince 4

Online

Additional photo tips:

- Be as feminine as possible, close to the line without being slutty
- Provide a variety of looks
- Show going out for the night

Headline ideas:

- Let's party, live life
- Run away, together, break away from it all
- Your perfect woman, at last

"About me" ideas:

- I am a nonconformist.
- I am bored by conventions of society; I need to break out somehow.
- I like to party.
- I have an interest in philosophy.
- I want to be the perfect woman to one lucky guy—all he will ever need.

"What I'm looking for in a man" ideas:

- Believes money and success aren't as important as enjoying life
- Wants connection, new experiences, parties
- Appreciates a woman of femininity
- Actually listens and "gets" me

"Dislikes" ideas:

- Being a conformist or a rule-follower
- Being one of the herd
- Those obsessing with money and "success" and are shallow

Offline

Probable jobs found in:

- Self-employed, transitory
- Hospitality industry
- Acting
- Where money is made with the least amount of hard work

Possible evening classes found at:

- Philosophy
- Entrepreneurship
- Acting

Visual clues:

- Ability to see into a woman's heart
- Casual dresser and demeanor
- Chivalrous to women
- Talks to women more than men (often as friends)
- Feels more comfortable around women than men; women gravitate toward him

Eavesdropping notes:

- Seeks places to go at night
- Wants sexual experiences
- Talks about women, past relationships
- Has disdain for money and being a slave to the system, yet, paradoxically, also talks about business ideas

Good ice breakers:

- A simple "hello" will be enough
- Any good places to go at night (ideally if you're new to the area)

Places commonly found:

- Bars, clubs, parties
- Gyms
- Hedonistic dating venues

Finding Prince 5

Online

Additional photo tips:

- Outdoors, wind in hair, girl next door
- Partying, at a bar
- Doing something adventurous

Headline ideas:

- Faithful and free
- Feel freedom, together, partners for adventures
- "Wendy" seeks her Peter Pan

"About me" ideas:

- I don't need all the trappings of life; I just need to get out and have fun.
- I don't want to chain a man down; we can be monogamous and have freedom.
- I love to play, joke around, travel, take adventure vacations.
- I don't know why so many people take life so seriously; it's no big deal.

"What I'm looking for in a man" ideas:

- Needs his alone time and gives me alone time too
- Is free-spirited and adventurous

- Wants to stay young with me forever
- Doesn't get uptight about things all the time; knows how to relax

"Dislikes" ideas:

- Monotony, boredom
- Debts and commitments, too much responsibility
- The corporate drone life

Offline

- Probable jobs found in:
- Self-employed, transient
- Fitness instructor, flying instructor, fisherman, park warden
- Actor
- Jobs with irregular hours and flexible schedule

Possible evening classes found at:

- N/A (This guy prefers to learn by picking up on snippets of what other people share.)

Visual clues:

- Casual clothing, shorts whenever possible
- Always on vacation, overtly playful, loud at times
- Shows a latent tension like a child feels when surrounded by adults
- Can appear lost or distracted, as though he needs looking after

Eavesdropping notes:

- Listening and learning, nodding head without much reply

- Enjoying adventures, party stories, dreams, and fantasies

- Speaking in a tense manner, trying to articulate something and not sound unintelligent

- Wanting to sound as capable and wise as everyone else

- Speaking snippets of wisdom that sound as though they came from someone else

Good ice breakers:

- As you grab a drink, "It's always five o'clock somewhere, right?"

- Reacting to something you both witnessed, someone getting upset, someone being late, and saying, "What's the big deal?"

- Praising him for something you witnessed him say or do.

Places commonly found:

- Casual "flip-flop" kind of bars

- Camping, hiking, beach, boating, outdoor life

Finding Prince 6

Online

Additional photo tips:

- Be as feminine as possible, close to the line without being slutty
- Partying, working out, cooking
- Watching a sports game
- Engaging in martial arts, extreme sports, something "white-knuckle" (if applicable)

Headline ideas:

- Any real men out there?
- Warrior wanted
- Heart rescue needed (This man wants to rescue a woman, so don't worry about not appearing to tick the E box when you talk about being rescued.)

"About me" ideas:

- I am spontaneous and adventurous.
- I like sports and going to sporting events.
- Look after me and I will look after you.
- I like cooking.

"What I'm looking for in a man" ideas:

- Being a "real" man, a man's man
- Can take care of a woman, protect her, come to her aid when she needs it

- Intelligent conversation not essential; let's party
- Wanting a party, not a "poet"

"Dislikes" ideas:

- Men not being men; acting with cowardice
- Being corporate drones
- Being a physically weak specimen

Offline

Probable jobs found in:

- Police, firefighter, paramedic
- Military
- Security business
- Fitness instructor, firearms instructor, lifeguard

Possible evening classes found at:

- Martial arts, firearms, etc.
- First aid
- Security guard qualifications

Visual clues:

- Seems on edge, on standby, on duty, ready to go
- Playing rough, being physical, playfully testing other males in a physical way

- Penetrating and shifting eyes
- Utilitarian clothing, combat pants or shorts, tight shirts

Eavesdropping notes:

- Quintessential guy-talk about beer, sports, games
- Daring people, pissing contests
- "Hell, yeah!" kind of speech
- Military versions quiet, more humble and pragmatic than nonmilitary

Good ice breakers:

- Giving fist-bumps when you hear him say something you approve of
- Commenting on sports and game action that create instant micro-communities
- Asking where he works out or what he's doing to work out
- Complimenting him: "Nice guns!"

Places commonly found:

- Sports bars close to police precincts or fire stations, preferably on big game days
- Gyms
- Gun stores, martial arts centers

Finding Prince 7

Online

Additional photo tips:

- A balance between very feminine and conservative elegance
- A variety of looks is essential
- One photo as if accompanying him to a ball or company dinner
- Background of a tidy and tasteful home

Headline ideas:

- Do not underestimate or question the usefulness of the word "king" in this situation!
- Queen seeks King
- Wing woman to a king, a king deserves the best, etc.
- All the woman you need and can handle, convey Assertiveness and Dignified as much as possible

"About me" ideas:

- I'm traditional, loyal, supportive, a team player.
- I've got your back.
- I'm clean, tidy, and organized.
- I enjoy being with family and hosting.
- I can take care of the emotional things that need handling.

"What I'm looking for in a man" ideas:

- Powerful man who takes charge
- Entrepreneurial type
- Man with big heart and big goals
- Wants the best in life for his family

"Dislikes" ideas:

- Overly emotional people
- Moochers, losers, entitled mentalities
- Disrespectful people
- People with no class or ambition

Offline

Probable jobs found in:

- Self-employed
- High level management, CEO

Possible evening classes found at:

- Anything, but he would feel more comfortable teaching the class

Visual clues:

- Big presence, highly sociable, works the room
- Appears to be the "mayor" of wherever he is as if he owns the place
- Appears to be in control and has all the answers

- People huddle around him
- Forcibly takes center stage, sits at middle of the bar not on the sidelines or a private corner
- Has a need to be seen
- Dresses smartly, wears an expensive watch
- Needs to convey a sense of power

Eavesdropping notes:

- Usually the loudest guy in the room
- Dominates the conversation and is advising people
- Wants extremely personal service from servers in restaurants
- Sensitive to anything perceived as disrespect

Good ice breakers:

- What do you do? What business are you in?
- What do you recommend on the menu?
- Any compliment that plays into and confirms the power he is trying to convey; his car, his suit, etc.
- Wants to be in charge, so let him.

Places commonly found:

- A workaholic, he's at work before and after hours.
- Conservative "steak and seafood" type establishments, the ones with an array of expensive cars outside
- Cigar bars (smoking cigars = "success")
- "Members only" places as exclusive as possible (e.g., golf clubs/courses, membership-required night spots, VIP lounges)

Important Prince 7 Note: Just in case all the glamor is swaying you toward considering Prince 7 as your match, be aware of an element of the Emperor's New Clothes. Some men might have the wealth, knowledge, and success they convey, but just as many are putting on a show (although in his heart he believes he has made it, which is what makes him so convincing).

In the Same Boat

We are engineering that magical moment instead of leaving it to chance. Knowing exactly what you want—and where and how to find it—puts you in the top percentile of people, especially in the dating world.

Your man is out there, as excited and nervous as you are. A man who is serious about dating is in the same boat as you. By taking the steps in Part Five, you're sailing straight for him. His soul is waiting for you to discover it like a pearl in an oyster. Now, it's time to open his shell.

Let's turn up the heat . . .

part six

CONTACT SPORT

One Jump Ahead

"The only thing we have to fear is fear itself—
nameless, unreasoning, unjustified terror which paralyzes
needed efforts to convert retreat into advance."

– FRANKLIN D. ROOSEVELT

Imagine the moment when you spot The One. What do you do about it? Let someone else take "your" man? You know who your preferred prince is, you know how to find him, and your next goal is to go on a first date with him. What are the odds of succeeding if left to the winds of chance?

We've already agreed it's time to write your own story—to take control of what's on offer. So, how will you get a date with him without coming across as a Husband-Seeking-Missile? Don't be so fast to laugh; another HSM has a much better chance than you do if your plan is to wait and wish that he selects *you*. At least she's trying.

Now that you know who your prince is, it should seem more non-sensical than ever to let guys do the choosing. The odds of a guy you like approaching you were already narrow. Thus, the odds of that guy also being your preferred prince is even narrower. You need to play *your* game with *your* rules if you want to win

As you'll see in the breakout session, different princes have different likelihoods of approaching you, so it's not as simple as saying, "Well, if a guy likes me, then he will approach me. If he doesn't, then he's lazy, and I don't want a lazy guy." Honestly, it has nothing to do with laziness. If you keep attracting the same kind of guy, it's probably because only certain male Genetypes have no qualms about speaking to a strange woman (you're a strange woman). And, incidentally, their effortless ability to do so also means the chances increase of your phone number being one of many on his phone. There is always a tradeoff. Some princes need more "handkerchiefs" dropped than others, and not all princes can be counted on to conveniently fit in with conventional dating "wisdom."

Of course, guys should make *some* effort. If this were a dating book for men I'd be kicking their asses so hard, they wouldn't be able to walk for weeks. But they aren't in the room with us, and we can't control what they do or don't do. We can only talk about what *you* will do—or not do.

So, we find ourselves at an impasse as we transition from finding him to winning a date with him. That is, unless we break away from the norm . . .

♛

Conventional wisdom says a man
has to make the first move. If you buy that,
then you are no longer writing your own story,
and that concept is entirely counter
to the principle of setting goals
to get what you want in life.

Who makes up these rules called "conventional wisdom" anyway? Maybe it was a guy who was confronted by an HSM. Or is there a Social Narrative Thinktank that convenes monthly to tell us what to do and how to think? Whatever, if it's not working for you, discard it.

♛

By definition,
a social narrative is herd behavior,
and when everyone is thinking the same thing,
nobody is thinking; they are bleating.

Remember James Bond and how guys love him? Don't women in Bond films always approach *him*? If you're smart, you'll start using this James Bond fantasy *for* you instead of *against* you. Women commonly believe they shouldn't approach a guy they like, yet that's exactly what's expected on a dating site. This is great for the proactive "Assertive" woman, you might say, but not for everyone. Not true.

Don't buy into the patriarchal narrative that tells you to stand against the wall and wait for a man to choose you. That's akin to the archaic principle of betrothal. If you want to be in control of your romantic story, then stay one jump ahead of the script. And, as you're about to see, "making a move" can merely mean giving a man well considered and measured signals, customized by prince type.

Don't worry, my guidance is with you all the way. Put me in your purse, call on me when you need me, and I shall grant you three wishes of assistance: The Approach, The Filter, and The Date. Let's begin with The Approach.

The Approach

You'll find two types of games in a casino: games of pure chance (like roulette) and games of probability (like blackjack). Professional gamblers, like professional traders, prefer games of probability, and consequently they abide by this basic principle:

Have a system and stick to it, be prepared for losses,
and understand that you have to lose some battles
to win the war. Continually play the odds, stay calm,
and don't throw your pacifier out of the stroller
at the first setback.

But it gets better for you, because you can do something that most professional gamblers can't: *you can see the dealer's hand.* You fill The Approach with the confidence that comes from a princess knowing something a prince doesn't: Genetypes.

The Approach – Online:

- Don't get lost in the digital world. Stay focused on your goals, which are: 1) Establish contact with suitable males, 2) Engage in a phone/text conversation with them away from the dating website as quickly as possible, 3) Apply The Filter, and 4) Go on a date in the real world. (Steps 3 and 4 are addressed in the next sections. The following points apply to 1 and 2.)

- Most women on dating sites don't take the initiative; instead, they rely on the (often numerous) initiatives from men. Don't be lazy about this. To use the incredible advantage of online dating, you can *and are expected to* approach as many guys as you like in a safe, nonembarrassing way. Make an effort. Lazy = unreliable, and no quality man wants a wife he can't count on. With online dating, you can and should allow yourself to veer toward the HSM side of the HSM—MIQ spectrum. It's a given you're online to find a man, and your enthusiasm can be infectious.

- Treat this Approach goal as you would any other goal, which means setting targets and creating routines. Users who go online frequently and most recently tend to get more attention, both from the site's algorithm and from CODE GREEN users wanting to find a woman who is serious and not flaky. So, check in every day (even if you don't take any action) to convey that you're serious. Next, set a weekly target of actual contacts you'll make, allowing for browsing time. Your week isn't over until you've reached that target.

- Interestingly, many people still prefer paperbacks to digital books, me included. Technology is great when it works, but when the wrong tool is used for the job at hand, it becomes more of a menace than anything. Recently, I was at a restaurant where, even though I could see servers everywhere, I had to order a margarita from my phone! One server standing in front of me refused to take my order. He and I shared a silent, surreal moment. Technology is supposed to make life easier, not harder, so when you find it's making your life harder, it's time to drop it. *Understand that the goal with online dating is to arrange an off-line date with your chosen prince as fast as possible.* After all, you aren't the only woman he's chatting to!

• If you think you've found your chosen type, take the trouble to write him a customized message so you stand out from the crowd. Lazily clicking on a "smile at John" button or sending him a lame "hi" doesn't cut it in terms of making an effort. Don't underestimate the power of appearing to single out one special person. Remember, men need to feel *adequate and useful.* (As you'll see, the breakout session offers specific ice breaker ideas for each prince.)

• When you come across male profiles, don't be too fast to judge, because you could be looking at a diamond in the rough. Most males online pretend to be a person they *think* females want to date. You can't assume anything, so apply only a basic filter of rejection before you've actually made contact—a filter like photos of him at a strip club.

The Approach – Offline:

For a society that's become besotted with the word "social," we live in a world where everything is either online or delivered to our door, so it's hardly any wonder we're not very social. Don't leave out engaging with people in the real world. The advantage? You can use your gut to assess *chemistry* as well as *compatibility.*

What is meant by The Approach in the off-line sense? It can be anything from giving a guy signals that you're interested to directly approaching him yourself. This gets more "seat of your pants" than online, but it's also more fun. Obviously, there are many places you could meet a guy in the real world, but let's focus on public evening spots such as bars and restaurants.

If I designed an establishment that ensured as little fraternization as possible between men and women, I would make it dark so people couldn't see each other well. To engage the men, I'd have large TV screens everywhere showing every sports event imaginable plus an antique car auction for good measure. Wait, I don't have to create such a place because it already exists: The Great American Bar. But at least those places are full of bodies. It's the other extreme in the land I come from—United Kingdom—where, in some dreary pub, you're grateful just to see your neighbor's dog. You're looking for what's between these extremes, because you need a good number of guys to be present *and* you need them to pay attention. The fewer sports on the TVs, the better.

Choose a large bar that has a rectangular or horseshoe-type design so people can face each other rather than a small bar where everyone faces a wall, and then follow these instructions:

• When you walk into a party or a bar, it's tempting to imagine all eyes on you, and this can be unnerving. Shine the light of truth on that classic self-conscious sensation by taking a good look around to see how many people actually *are* looking. If indeed they are, make brief eye contact, smile if you feel the need, then take a seat. By now, the fear has dissipated, and everyone knows a WANTED woman just walked in. That creates a show of confidence.

- Do not enter the bar accompanied by another man, even if he's gay. That tells the single men in there, "Stay away, I'm taken." It's okay to go with another couple—very powerful, actually, if it appears you need a date—but make it blatantly clear you are the one who's not with the guy. (You might see a situation in which both women act as if they're with the same guy, even though one is single. This happens a lot.) Ideally, it's you and one girlfriend; any more than one can feel intimidating for a guy who wants to approach you.

- Most men don't read body language the same way most women do. This contributes to why many women don't understand the reason a man doesn't approach them—even after they've given him several signals that are obvious to other women but not most men. That means you have to help him notice you more than you think, depending on your chosen prince's disposition. (The breakout session provides a "handkerchief rating" to indicate how obvious and frequent your signals need to be with each prince. The rating's name refers to Victorian-era ladies dropping a handkerchief in the path of a gentleman of interest, thus giving him the green light to approach them.)

- Sit at the area of the bar where most people have to pass to get to the restroom. Arrive early if you have to, and *own that real estate*. At some point when people visit the restroom, this bottleneck creates the most risk-free opportunities for first contact. You're creating a low-pressure, low-risk, "just-passing" situation as opposed to everyone at the bar knowing one of you is making a move.

- You might ask, "But if a guy likes the look of you, won't he just walk over?" First, the problem lies with the question, which is based purely on his looks and his watch stuck on Primal Time. Second, it depends on the Genetype, but even the most forward prince types can feel intimidated if a real thunderbolt moment hits. Actually, the more a guy likes you, the more it feels like someone poured concrete on his feet. That combines with dreaded male pride and his fear of not being adequate. There's also the possibility that he's living out the James Bond fantasy, staying put, playing it cool as he sips his "shaken, not stirred" martini. (By the way, to have a bit of ice-breaking fun with "Mr. Bond" over there, politely joke that the afficionado's way to drink a martini is "stirred, not shaken" because shaking the vodka over ice "bruises" it.)

- Do you recall our discussion about male pride and his need to feel adequate? In a public setting like a bar, this can manifest as *fear of rejection*, depending on his prince profile. This fear can become so great that his perceived risk of rejection outweighs his perceived value of winning you as a mate. The more guy friends he's with, the worse this can be because of the hierarchical nature of the male world where men unconsciously compete over who is most *useful*. (This is partly where the obsession with trophies such as cars and watches comes from—both commonly featured in Bond films.) Bear in mind that it's not as simple as "just walking over to say hi."

- Add into the mix that we live in a fear culture in which many men feel unsure about what's appropriate or not—even basic rituals such as approaching a woman. As an active women's rights supporter, I heartily further female empowerment through actions and words, but let's consider the trade-off. With more power comes more responsibility, and, in the dating world, this responsibility requires women to take more initiative.

• Most guys have been burned at some point by women giving them obvious signals, only to be laughed at or promptly dismissed by the "lady" in question. Two female Genetypes can be guilty of this. One does it for attention or to spark a confrontation with her soon-to-be-present boyfriend, and another one does it for mindless conquest. In both cases, that discourages men from ever speaking to women. You know if it's you I'm talking about, *and* you now know what you're doing to both men and women. Don't be a bitch—karma is an even bigger bitch.

• When you've finally engaged with a guy, don't be a lame conversationalist or come across as being "hard work." Your day was never merely "good"; you are never merely "fine." Instead of one-word responses, elaborate, converse. Thanks to smart phones and technology, it seems people have lost the art of verbal conversation. Thousands of years in the future, perhaps we will have evolved into beings with no tongues and stylus-shaped thumbs. But until then, take your head out of your phone (= "I'm too busy to speak to you") and *engage* with your fellow humans.

Approach Signals

Let's talk about what signals to make The Approach with. I suggest four levels. Their usage needs to take into account the prince-profile in question, how distracting the environment is, and how effective your current efforts are. In order of boldness, the four levels are: 1) The Look, 2) The Wave, 3) The Ice Break, and 4) The Nuclear Option.

1) The Look

You should already be familiar with that moment of eye contact, but again, it's about being in the middle of that spectrum between HSM and MIQ. First, make sure to consider the visual cues of the prince you're looking for and not be distracted by eye candy based on Primal Time thinking (as noted earlier). Next, adopt two stages to The Look: an initial glance that holds eye contact for about a second (= "I see you"), then after a pause, a second lock of eyes for a few seconds accompanied by a friendly smile (= "I like you"). If that fails and/or your prince has a higher Handkerchief Rating, move on to step two.

2) The Wave

This has always worked well for me: Smiling, then waving at someone as if you know that person. One advantage of The Wave is you can do it from great distance if required. But do it as soon as you notice the person; otherwise, it loses the effect of seeming like he's already an acquaintance. As a guy when I use this technique, half the time the woman would approach me. That tells me the effect of The Wave on a guy who waits for a handkerchief drop will be even greater. You risk little embarrassment or motion with The Wave, yet you're giving him a big, fat green light to "just come over." If he approaches you and asks, "Do I know you?" just say, "You seem familiar. Anyway, my name is . . ." If that fails and/or if your prince has a higher Handkerchief Rating, move on to step three.

3) The Ice Break

In the breakout session, you'll find specific ice breakers customized for each of the princes. Because they are designed to resonate with a specific profile, they have the additional purpose of an early-stage filter. To break the ice, first be clear what you're going to say. Second, position yourself as naturally close to him as possible (e.g., ordering a drink at the bar—also a great eavesdropping opportunity as he passes you on the way to restroom). Ideally, he's already within talking range. As you'll see in the list of ice breakers, there is little risk of rejection; it's one human being making polite (but prince-specific!) conversation with another. If that fails and/or if your prince has a higher Handkerchief Rating, move on to step four . . .

4) The Nuclear Option

Sometimes, you have to go nuclear, but keep this as your ultimate weapon to be used sparingly for emergencies. What constitutes an emergency? You appear to have both a compatibility and chemistry match, all other options have failed, and it's the final few minutes of game time. Women have used this on me a few times. On each of those occasions, I hadn't noticed her before she made this move. And on each of those occasions, I subsequently went on a date with her *because she executed it the right way, the classy way.* Here's what you do: discreetly write your name and phone number on a scrap of paper or use a business card if you have one. Pass him on the way to the restroom and say, "We're both busy with friends tonight, but you seem really nice. Here's my number, call me. Have a great night." Then walk away

and get on with your evening *without giving him any more
handkerchiefs.* Completely ignore him, actually; you've done
enough. If he comes over, great. If he calls you, great. This
is a tactic men can use, but they rarely enjoy much success
with it, so use this option to your advantage. If the Nuclear
Option fails, then at least you have no regrets for not trying.
Perhaps you'll even make a new friend or two along the way.
But let's discuss this a little more because, as powerful as it is,
it's something most women need extra coaching to execute.
Remember how men need to feel adequate? Can you imagine
how much you've boosted his male pride by walking over
there like that—*especially* if he's with his friends, who will now
think he's a "stud." So, don't feel intimidated. The Nuclear
move is a *huge* compliment to a man, even if he doesn't feel
the same as you. He may suddenly become interested in you
when he wasn't before. Forget that he might be The One or
that thought will make you nervous. Just see him as a fellow
human. Convey only that you're a WANTED, especially
"Assertive" single woman who is being sociable. A trick
public speakers use if they're feeling nervous is to imagine
audience members sitting on the toilet, so why not use it
here? This imagery will relax you and even make you grin.

The Filter

At this point, you've found potentially suitable men and have
possibly exchanged contact details with them, either offline or
online. If offline, you probably know if there's chemistry or not;
if online, that is still to be checked. But in both cases, it's time to
apply The Filter. Remember, it's a two-stage filter: 1) eliminate players

(time-waster filter) and 2) discover if he is your chosen prince profile (compatibility filter). *Compatibility + Chemistry = Life Partner.*

Part Four told you how to spot and deal with players and undesir-
ables, so let's discuss a filter for them with the following:

- Where is one of the best places for CODE RED guys to find
  women? Yes, dating sites. Now that you're aware of how to
  handle these men, apply what you know to the online world
  as best you can. (This advice by no means discounts the huge
  advantages of online dating.)

- Be safe and undeterred by any weirdos or haters you see on
  the dating site. The internet suddenly gave self-loathing
  individuals and nut jobs a way to be heard, and they're making
  up for lost time. Don't take anything personally; some people
  just want to watch the world burn. We wish them peace.

- Don't worry about giving your contact details to people,
  because you can block anyone at the touch of a button.
  Online, consider using Skype to chat. There, all people have
  is a username, not a phone number, and you can also block
  any users you don't want or even report them. Also with Skype,
  you can video call a guy at random (but not unreasonable)
  times to see if he'll answer. It's best to call outside work hours
  when he'd have fewer excuses not to pick up. Why do this?
  Because if he's married or attached or a player, he likely won't
  pick up. Don't get too crazy or suspicious, though. Give him
  the benefit of the doubt while being persistent with your
  video calls. It must be video, because anyone can hide behind
  a text or a phone call. Also, remember that with texting, you
  can't detect a person's tone. Looking into someone's eyes tells
  you if that person is sincere.

- Take your prince's profile into account when assessing if he's a player or not. For example, Prince 5 feels very comfortable around women and enjoys talking to them. Prince 4 is driven by a need to feel free, which is not to be confused with being a commitment-phobe.

- When it comes to arranging a date, make it a weekend. This is another player trap; men already living with someone are typically expected to be with them on the weekends, so, unless he clearly works weekends, a player continually avoids weekend dates.

More online pointers for The Filter:

- Remember, when online, you don't have the advantage of your senses and gut feelings; photos can be deceptive, as can words. You're taking a great deal on faith, so don't get too involved with someone online before you've had a chance to meet him, and then let your senses take over.

- That's not to say we aren't going to use the online world as a filter to make sure you won't even *go* on a first date with a type you know is incompatible. But many women will text a guy on the site indefinitely; meanwhile, a smart woman takes him away from the dating site and onto an app like Skype. I won't get tired of saying this: *the sole purpose of online dating is to secure a first date in the real world.* You aren't there to find pen pals! Do you want a pen pal or a life partner? You can't have a relationship with your phone (even if it is set to vibrate).

- Next, let's apply the Genetype filter to check for the all-important compatibility factor. Is this guy your chosen prince or not?

Your aim is to not even go on a first date
until you're 90 percent certain
he's your chosen type.

If you and he met online, you could accomplish this by text and video chat before going on a date. However, there's no harm in moving straight to the first date so you can check both for compatibility and chemistry. Assessing his Genetype is *much* easier in person. And if you met him offline, you want to see about the compatibility on top of the chemistry you evidently experienced during The Approach. In all cases, the process is the same:

You need to quickly but casually
figure out which prince he is,
using what appears to be
everyday conversation.

Here's how . . .

- You *must* know his prince profile like the back of your hand. The hazard? You have a preconceived idea of what type you *hope* this guy is. Make sure you're being objective and that *confirmation bias* isn't getting in the way of your assessment. This is especially important if you're highly attracted to him and feel positive chemistry. That's when you'll *want* this guy to fit the profile. But confirmation bias will work against you if you ignore all the flags that would dismiss your assessment.

- With practice, you'll notice that appearances and energy can be seen between certain Genetypes before they've said a word, so get a feel for the typical appearance of your chosen prince. (See breakout session in Part Five for visual cues.) Practice as much as possible, ideally on friends and relatives.

Once you two are talking, use your newfound powers—and here's when the magic begins . . .

While he's on Primal Time, begin a conversation that's far more stimulating than the usual banality. This makes you more appealing and interested in him at a deep level as you dig out his soul (= "Hey, this girl is kind of cool; she's not like the rest. She seems interested in who I am; I feel adequate.")

The trick is to identify his
Dominant Driver as quickly as possible
(listed in Part Two).

Do not load this initial question. To explain what that means, let's use Prince 3 as an example. Prince 3's Dominant Driver is creativity, so loading this question to him would be to say, "So, are you a really creative person?" or, even worse, "You're really creative, right?" Lots of people are creative, not only Prince 3, so many different prince types could answer yes to that question. Oops. You're now off in the wrong direction. The difference is that Prince 3 is *centered* around creativity; it's what he is *compelled* to do, and joy becomes his reward for doing it.

Now, keep your mind open to the possibility he's *not* Prince 3 by looking him straight in the eye and asking this magical question:

♛

"What ONE thing brings you
the most JOY?"

Don't settle for an answer that confuses pleasure with joy. We can all enjoy the pleasure of good food, for example. Joy resides on another level; it's spiritual and bittersweet, a lot like love. Which raises another good question:

♛

"In your spare time,
what ONE thing do you most LOVE to do?"

Follow this question with:

"WHY do you love that so much?"
"How does it make you FEEL?"
"What is your DREAM in life?"

Now you're speaking to his soul. If you're listening carefully, asking about a person's favorite film/book can tell you a lot. Asking what he dreams about doing is another probing question. Watch closely for the moments when the conversation makes his eyes widen. That's when you can peer into his soul (aka Genetype).

Let's run a simulation that deliberately creates a worst-case scenario for training purposes. In this example, a woman named Jane has previously chosen Prince 4 as her match. In a bar one evening, Jane has identified a guy, John, whom she seems to have chemistry with. She's already broken the ice with The Wave and now tries to assess if John is indeed a Prince 4. John is busy trying to look "adequate" or cool in front of Jane, thus unconsciously creating a smokescreen to his true nature.

> *Jane: "So, John, what one thing brings you the most joy?"*

> *John (laughing, holding up his whiskey glass): "Wow, great question! I guess you're looking at it. Great times, having fun, hanging out. How about you?"*

At this juncture, the danger for Jane is confirmation bias. Prince 4 does indeed enjoy the party life, but so do a lot of guys. John's somewhat nervous response is common and not considered enough evidence. Still, she shouldn't rule out the possibility of him being a Prince 4. The fact that John asked the question back to Jane could also be a Prince 4 flag (being particularly interested in and comfortable around women), but we still don't have enough to go on. Continuing the simulation . . .

> *Jane: "I love spending my spare time in nature. What do you love doing most in your spare time?"*

Good job, Jane, keep batting the ball right back to John . . .

> *John (his eyes widen a little, his enthusiasm steps up a gear): "Oh, yes. I love nature too. The water, you know, and sunsets. Have you ever seen the sunset at Key West? Oh, it's so beautiful, I just sit and watch the whole thing . . ." John's eyes glaze over and shift. He continues, "Yeah, bought myself some investment property down there, flipped a quick profit, I can tell you!"*

Mixed signals plus a sign of bullshit going on somewhere. Jane seemed to touch his soul with her comment about nature. Afterward, she noticed him drift off, becoming romantic and poetic, his eyes widening, his hands becoming animated and emphatic as he described the sunset, absorbed by his "poem." Then, something changed, and he became more concerned with money, which could also indicate he was a Prince 7, but Jane could see his eyes were no longer widened; money and power wasn't driving him as it would a Prince 7.

At this point, do not lose eye contact. Eyes are the windows to a person's soul, yes, but those windows have the curtains closed until you SPEAK to a person's soul. You know what I'm talking about. You intuitively *know* when someone comes to life.

Jane smiles and nods, pausing for thought as she slowly reaches for her drink and takes a sip. Time for a little elimination: This guy is too emotional and poetic to be a Prince 1 (logical, black and white) or a Prince 6 (more physical than verbal and poetic) or a Prince 7 (sees emotions as weakness). That leaves Princes 2 (knowledge), 3 (creativity), 5 (freedom), or her sought-after 4 (philosophy) as possibilities.

> Jane: *"Well done on that property flip! So, does that make you more of an indoors or an outdoors person?"*

Praise him whenever the opportunity presents itself, and do so sincerely. Next, Jane continues her process of eliminating as she probes to see if he's a reclusive Prince 2 or an outdoors/freedom-loving Prince 5. But she doesn't get much of a reaction from John's eyes and energy. Then he says:

John: "Sea and sunsets, yes, beautiful. South California,
mountains behind you and sunset over the sea in front of
you, awesome. You know, there's this place where . . ."

As John drifts off again with his "painting," Jane rightfully rules
out Prince 2. And Prince 5 would be talking more about *doing*
things on the beach or in the mountains, so she rightfully sidelines
that option. John hasn't yet asked much about Jane, and a Prince 4
would be asking more about her by now. This guy seems more like
a Prince 3 (creativity). Jane asserts her original question:

Jane: "So what DO you love doing in your spare time?"

John: "Reading. Yeah, I've got a great idea for writing a
book, actually. Love to cook, too."

Jane: "So, creativity is what brings you most joy?"

At this point, it's okay for Jane to load her question because it's not
her first one, and she's basing it on what John just indicated. She
seeks to eliminate him as a Prince 3. She knows that if Prince 4 raves
about anything, it would be going out, partying, or working on
an entrepreneurial dream (unconvincingly). Then John's eyes widen
again, as if something Jane said lifts his spirit and focuses him.

John: "Yes! I think so. Never really gave it much thought,
but yes, being creative."

Boom. Prince 3.

Jane: "Awesome! Good luck with that book. Well, John, it
was a pleasure meeting you, and I'm sure I'll see you in here
again. Always great to meet interesting people, and a person
can never have too many friends."

With this polite and encouraging no from Jane, her final line told John they're "only friends" from this moment on. That way, it won't be awkward when they next bump into each other. John's male pride remains intact (so he won't go around saying she's a flirt, etc.), and he becomes another social contact who may have social events to invite Jane to with suitable Prince 4 friends.

After this interaction, all is good on Planet Dating, despite it not going exactly as Jane had hoped. You'll see I deliberately created a tough example. Worst case, had Jane not been sure which prince John was, what would be the harm in going on a date away from the bravado of the bar scene when his guard would be down? She'd simply have more time to find out.

Be aware that most people won't simply blurt out their Dominant Driver (listed for each prince in Part Two) when asked what one thing brings them the most joy. In fact, most don't *know* the answer because they've never consciously thought about it; they simply have a deep yearning for "something." (It's their true spirit—their gut—trying to awaken them.) You may have to coax people's inner truth out of them, as Jane had to with John, but usually people pause for reflection and then use language that *describes* what brings them deep joy. For example, Prince 1 isn't going to reply, "Logic!" to the magic question; he'll use descriptors such as "solving problems, organizing, and getting the job done." (In the breakout session, you'll see listed "Possible Driver Descriptors" for each prince.)

To further hit home an important point from the simulation, every prince possesses *some* of all the qualities of the other princes. All guys can be a *little* logical, knowledge-seeking, creative, philosophical, freedom-loving, protective, and power-seeking, maybe even a *lot*.

However . . .

What defines a Dominant Driver
is COMPULSION.

Staying on the example of a Prince 3 (creativity), sure, all guys can be creative, but they are not *compelled* to be. They won't usually lose sleep over a creative project that may or may not be profitable.

Unless we embrace our God-given Dominant Driver—our true purpose in life—the soul will not be at peace. Conversely, when we embrace this purpose, the soul comes to life, and we are connected to The Divine. A Dominant Driver is the sun in our personal solar system, and that sun's rays burst through our eyes when the clouds are swept back. (For more learning simulations and to share your scenarios, go to www.JamesSheridan.com/KFFsimulator.)

Jane may have just saved two years of her life finding out the hard way that John wasn't compatible. Perhaps she'd even face a divorce (assuming she had correctly chosen Prince 4 as her compatibility match). She never even had to go on a date with the guy to know he wasn't The One because, although she felt chemistry, she learned there was no compatibility. Remember:

Compatibility + Chemistry = Life Partner

What about poor John, though? As well as working for her own agenda, Jane was literally soul-searching on John's behalf. She may have sparked an awakening in him that would lead to great things as John pursues his true purpose. *And this is the power you take to your new relationship when you do find The One,* as Jane surely will. When Jane finds her Prince 4, and she awakens and supports him in this way, that Prince 4 will feel extremely *useful and adequate,* deeply loved and cared for, in a relationship with a woman the likes of which he's never encountered.

Sure, Jane had to do some homework. She read this book thoroughly (I love her), especially learning all the male profiles. She took this time to learn a life skill that won't only help her romantically but professionally, too. When interacting with a client/boss/colleague, male or female, she will know the right buttons to push. (Remember, *The You Code* also lists all the female types for your reference.)

I often hear people complain that they "don't have the time" to do certain things, but isn't it worthwhile when the prize awaits you and pain is avoided? Plus, people seem to find time for social media, TV shows, waiting in line for a "coffee" that's like an ice cream sundae, and, yes, bitching about their love life. I tell clients, "Well, in that case, *create* time by getting up an hour earlier and going to bed an hour later (sober), and you'll gain an extra fourteen hours each week." That's when they suddenly find time to study these Genetypes. How strange.

Please know this:

One of your most important decisions in life
is who you choose to share it with—forever.

So, master the art of making this one-time decision
wisely.

Guess what? Since we've been talking, Jane met another guy who is, it seems, a Prince 4 and both a chemistry and a compatibility match. (Damn, this girl is fast—and not in a bad way.) So, now it's time for . . .

The Date

The more we progress, the more we can take off the training wheels and let nature take its course, or it gets too mechanical—and that maybe makes you nervous. As long as you can see both chemistry and Genetypal compatibility, then my work is largely done (other than making a speech at your wedding). But don't worry, I'm still looking out for you. You've been on dates before, you know the drill, so just let me offer a few pointers here. (The info in the breakout session is the most important part about the first date, which is when misunderstandings can arise.)

- Stay focused on the next goal: *the goal of the first date is to explore compatibility + chemistry and, if confirmed, to secure a second date.*

- Don't forget everything we've talked about so far, including staying WANTED when arranging the date, during it, and after it. Don't chase too much—that is, if you're texting more than he is, you're chasing.

- Choose a suitable venue, ideally tailored to each prince, as another great way to bond with him (more of this in the breakout session). But, in all cases, choose a venue that allows conversation! Don't forget that, for online-sourced princes, the first date is when you need to check for chemistry. For offline-sourced princes, the first date is an opportunity to double-check your assessment. In any case, you're making a deeper connection, so why would you want to spend it staring at a movie screen together?

• Be safe. Choose a venue that's a highly public place, ideally a bar or restaurant that has valet parking, so you can drive up to the door and hand the keys to the valet at the entrance. This way, there is no "parking lot risk." But, don't get paranoid either and go into the date believing there's a 50/50 chance he's a serial killer. That won't exactly give off the right vibe.

• "It's a woman's prerogative to be late" is a phrase originally coined by women who can't be bothered to keep track of time. You know how long it takes to get ready, because you do it all the time before work. I get it, it's uncomfortable to sit at a bar alone as you wait for a date while gawking men assume you're there for a one-night stand. Being an hour early stinks of HSM to your date, so a ten- to fifteen-minute grace period is acceptable to most men. But being too late without a major reason = flake = untrustworthy. Definitely not the behavior of a WANTED woman who is in a permanent state of "hooya!" Customize your arrival time to the mentality of your chosen prince. Taking the two extreme examples, Prince 1 will arrive early while Prince 5 can be counted on to be late for absolutely no reason, and he means no disrespect by it. He thinks, "What's the big deal?" (More in the breakout session.)

• If you happen to notice his fancy car, don't be fooled. People can get a car loan anywhere these days. Same goes for his watch and clothes, even his house. In the Land of Credit, it's

all a month-to-month illusion. Most important, ask yourself
if material possessions are more important to you than true
love and deep connection with a partner.

- No matter his prince profile, he is likely also nervous. The
more he likes you, the more nervous he is—and tongue-tied.
So, make allowances for both him and you. Laugh about
something together as soon as possible. This is a great public
speaking trick: getting a laugh early in the speech creates an
early bond with the audience while also relaxing the speaker.
Please, just don't make it a knock-knock joke . . .

- Whether checking for chemistry (online-sourced date) or
double-checking for compatibility (offline-sourced date), use
the soul-searching techniques previously discussed, but don't
make it feel like you're interviewing the poor guy.

- If he seems awesome, keep your fears and doubts in check!
As seen in the simulation notes of John's and Jane's encounter,
you can truly believe he can't do better than you!

- On Jane's date, Prince 5 says, "I'm not looking for anything
serious." Jane replies, "Oh, and here's me wondering at what
point tonight you were going to propose to me!" Get a laugh,
relax both you and him, and understand that he may still be on
Primal Time and/or nervous and/or frightened about divorcing
his James Bond fantasy—or losing his freedom. You've also
countered his remark by politely conveying, "I don't need you
either, buddy!" This common remark by a guy can also mean
he's so taken with you that it scares him. Whatever. The main
thing is for you to stay WANTED. Let the evening progress
naturally by quickly diffusing his throwaway comment and

allowing you both to relax. Remember, we agreed that being a player involves an element of willful deceit, so this remark —"I'm not looking for anything serious"—doesn't qualify in this case. But a player might also use this comment to see what you'll put up with. Remember, as long as a player's goal-posts are removed, he can't win his game. Plus, measure this remark in the context of the prince you're with.

• As for the rest of the date, relax and enjoy yourself. Yeah. You have a compatibility and chemistry match! Stay WANTED. Feel with your heart instead of judging with your (prejudiced) head, and let the Universe show you the way. Remember from Part Three: *every time is the first time.*

A Whole New World

Let's address specifics about the breakout session with these points:

• A Handkerchief Rating has been given to each prince to indicate the number/boldness of signals you likely need to give your prince on a scale of 1 to 5, with 1 being the lowest amount of signaling likely needed. Again, I can only offer likelihoods and probabilities; depending on the situation, any prince could need any number of signals, but this indicates an intelligent guess.

• Suitable Ice Breakers are tips to follow.

• Driver Descriptors are attached to each prince to give you the type of answers he's likely to provide when you ask, "What brings you the most joy?"

• Tardiness Tolerance gives you an idea of his possible tardiness on the date, so you can take his profile into account before judging. It's on a scale of 1 to 5, with 5 being the most inclined to tardiness. This also indicates how tolerant he will be over your being tardy.

• Venue Ideas go beyond the assumed bar setting, so apply these to further dates. But if it's a first date, then ensure you can follow the safety rules as much as possible.

• "His favorite letter in WANTED" indicates his probable priority in a partner. He still needs all the letters, but each type puts one at the top of his list.

Dating Prince 1:

The Approach

HANDKERCHIEF RATING: 4

SUITABLE ICE BREAKERS:

- Anything that pertains to his profession such as requests for professional advice
- Who is currently hiring for management or professionals in the area
- Useful tips for networking, recruitment, plus suggestions for business apps, perhaps triggered by a problem he was discussing

Notes: He works much like a computer, assessing facts, interpreting, and calculating the response. So, it's sensible to make your "input" as simple and unambiguous as possible. Insinuation, abstraction, suggestion, indirect speech aren't the best methods. Say what you mean and be prepared to step it up with the handkerchiefs.

The Filter

DRIVER DESCRIPTORS: Solving problems, organizing, getting the job done, resolving issues

Notes: This type can be found in many jobs, so don't let what he does lead you in any one direction. He will appreciate your focusing on his specialist subject—his career—so steer him away from the details of that. Instead, pull out what he likes most about his work or a particular aspect of it. If he says that what brings him the most joy is working, dig deeper because many people might say that. Your immediate next question is to ask *what* he loves most about his work, and keep digging.

The Date

VENUE IDEAS: Conventional places such as bars and restaurants
to keep it simple

TARDINESS TOLERANCE: 1

HIS FAVORITE LETTER IN WANTED: A

Notes: Take the initiative with the first conversation, talk about
work, and he will relax and have a great time. Expect some silence.
Keep your conversation literal and direct.

Dating Prince 2:

The Approach

HANDKERCHIEF RATING: 4

SUITABLE ICE BREAKERS:

- Book recommendations, ask what book he has in his hand

- Commenting on mutually witnessed herd behavior

- Unusual travel destinations you might spark a conversation
  about

Notes: His favorite place is his home, so be prepared to meet this
guy anywhere and improvise. The sooner you can make a connection
through sharing some of your knowledge or asking about one of his
special interests, the better. As early as possible, ask what his hobbies
are, what he does, etc. Until proven otherwise, you are just another
one of the mindless masses, so make an impression quickly by
saying something that isn't mundane or pointless.

The Filter

DRIVER DESCRIPTORS: learning new skills, reading, teaching

Notes: When you ask what brings him the most joy, be prepared for him to zoom in and tell you about his "flavor of the month" special interest. But that's not what *you* are looking for; you need to zoom out and see the bigger picture, the sum of the parts.

The Date

VENUE IDEAS: Museum, nature, unusual places like a temple, keep it quiet, interesting, and bohemian. Extra points if it's based on one of his eclectic range of interests.

TARDINESS TOLERANCE: 2

HIS FAVORITE LETTER IN WANTED: E

Notes: If the venue is chosen wisely, all should go well. He will feel relaxed, and you will have an opportunity to bond. Find a way to show (not tell) that you also like having your space and you need your alone time.

Dating Prince 3:

The Approach

HANDKERCHIEF RATING: 2–4, depending on the mood and/ or how deep into a project he is

SUITABLE ICE BREAKERS:
- If possible, praise his work (huge)
- Enter on a creative discussion just overheard, "Cool, what if . . ."
- Comment on mutually witnessed herd mentality

Notes: He's used to random people approaching him, so don't worry. The more cogs you see turning in his head, the more handkerchiefs you'll need. If he's deep into something, it's a genuine tradeoff for him to balance losing his connection with The Muse against making the effort to approach a woman he likes, even someone as WANTED as you.

The Filter

DRIVER DESCRIPTORS: some kind of artistic activity he's into such as writing, cooking, painting, music, art, presentations, making things, coming up with new ideas and inventions

Notes: Don't be tempted to use what someone does for a job as the big clue about their type. This guy, in particular, likely came up against too many barriers to pursue his true joy of being a creative artist due to competition, bad or risky pay, and society giving him different messages. The simulation we did earlier is a good example of how this works. His true joy may be buried deep down. But compensating for it is that he says what he thinks and wears his heart on his sleeve, so his joy is easily witnessed when triggered. An abstract concept like "joy" appeals to him.

The Date

VENUE IDEAS: nature, whatever art he most enjoys but nothing noisy where it's hard to talk, inspirational venues featuring grand or unusual architecture, wine tasting, paintings, etc.

TARDINESS TOLERANCE: 3

HIS FAVORITE LETTER IN WANTED: T

Notes: If he's created something artistic, his dream date would be where his artistry was on display, not to be egotistical, but rather to appreciate and acknowledge his work (don't confuse these two things). Don't consider him impolite if he quickly shifts conversations away from what you were talking about. Remember, he speaks what's on his mind. People tend to think things they don't really mean, and their thoughts are fleeting, but he might actually come out with it.

Dating Prince 4:

The Approach

HANDKERCHIEF RATING: 1

SUITABLE ICE BREAKERS:

- A simple "hello" will be enough
- Any good places to go at night (ideally if you're fairly new to the area)

Notes: He will try to talk about you, but shift the conversation back onto him.

The Filter

DRIVER DESCRIPTORS: enjoying the moment, partying and going out, looking at the world in a different way, escaping, breaking out of the system

Notes: His core purpose of philosophy is buried deep, so don't expect him to answer your question on his joy in any way close to "philosophy." You'll need to use a combination of clues, including his profile, visual cues, and a process of elimination—that is, what he's *not*. This does mean, though, that his awakening will be all the more powerful when it comes, and you can be its deliverer.

The Date

VENUE IDEAS: Speakeasy bars or restaurants, let him choose

TARDINESS TOLERANCE: 4

HIS FAVORITE LETTER IN WANTED: W

Notes: He will be comfortable, so just relax and go with the flow. Assess if he's looking for a serious relationship. Support his career/financial aspirations, but don't get too excited about the status or money expected to result. Make your encounter more, well, philosophical.

Dating Prince 5:

The Approach

HANDKERCHIEF RATING: 3

SUITABLE ICE BREAKERS:

- As you grab a drink, say, "It's always five o'clock somewhere, right?"
- Reacting to something you both witnessed, probably someone getting unnecessarily upset about something or being late, thinking, "What's the big deal?"
- Praising him for something you witnessed him say or do

Notes: Relax, keep it casual. Coming across too officious will really blow it with him.

The Filter

DRIVER DESCRIPTORS: doing whatever I want each day, being outdoors, adventurous, feeling free

Notes: Expect resistance from him as you dig. The more obvious it is you're figuring him out, the harder it will be. This stems from a latent insecurity about not acting how most of society wants men to act (career/goal driven), and the conversation can suddenly take a tense turn, with palpable defensiveness. The good news? It's not that difficult to see if freedom is his Dominant Driver, even if he doesn't directly say so.

The Date

VENUE IDEAS: fishing, any adventure where you aren't separated or it's too intense or noisy to talk, beach bars. Dress informally, keeping it casual and without ceremony.

TARDINESS TOLERANCE: 5

HIS FAVORITE LETTER IN WANTED: A and E

Notes: A woman who takes charge can appeal to him; he thinks she can make the decisions for him. Indicate how much your life allows him alone time. Say how it's possible to be in a monogamous relationship and still enjoy freedom, either together or individually.

Dating Prince 6:

The Approach

HANDKERCHIEF RATING: 2–4, depending on the situation

SUITABLE ICE BREAKERS:

- Fist-bump when you hear or see him say something you approve of.

- Sports games create instant micro-communities, so comment on some game action.

- Ask where he works out or what he's doing to work out, and say, "Nice guns."

Notes: Balance the need for handkerchiefs on how many guys he's with and what the setting is. He's a literal man—a "man's man"—so his fearlessness and overt masculinity can be hobbled by *not* having his male pride hurt in front of his friends. This also means his pride will be all the more pumped for you going bold with the handkerchiefs and singling him out, especially if his friends also see you drop them.

The Filter

DRIVER DESCRIPTORS: action, working out, making a difference, saving lives, service, and duty

Notes: This man is not usually a deep thinker, and he doesn't do well with abstract ideas, so he's inclined to confuse joy with pleasures like beer, food, and women. This means you'll have to do the work and/or make your assessment more a sum of the parts of his profile and visual cues, plus how he feels about his occupation. If he has a desk job, he'll be unenthused. It's okay to ask him what brings him joy, but be prepared to quickly move on; for example, ask what he'd love to do most if he were capable of doing anything.

The Date

VENUE IDEAS: stadium tour or sports hall of fame (instead of a sports event), but stay away from sports bars! Choose an outdoor activity venue that isn't too noisy and doesn't separate you. Make sure it at least gives you the opportunity to have a drink over a "debrief" (e.g., an amusement park with white-knuckle rides and/ or challenges of physical skill).

TARDINESS TOLERANCE: 2

HIS FAVORITE LETTER IN WANTED: W

Notes: What you see is what you get. He's a simple man who enjoys simple pleasures and lives for the physical more than the mental. Sharing action and adrenaline is enough for him to bond with you. Making early advances could be expected, so appreciate that he's usually more inclined to Primal Time than other types.

Dating Prince 7:

The Approach

HANDKERCHIEF RATING: 1 (assuming he's not distracted)

SUITABLE ICE BREAKERS:
- Any compliment that plays into and confirms the power he is trying to convey (e.g., his car, his suit, etc.)
- "What do you do? What business are you in?"

- "What do you recommend on the menu here?" He wants to be in charge, so let him.

Notes: He is usually working the room, at least in one pocket of it, so look as womanly as possible, and be prepared to compete for his attention. Hold him in your spot. He will stay as long as he feels respected and is talking about himself. If he's getting too much attention from other women, be prepared to go nuclear.

The Filter

DRIVER DESCRIPTORS: success, winning a deal, buying a car or house, having his own business

Notes: This type is usually obvious based on previous notes in this book. However, be sure not to confuse Prince 7 with an A-type personality (aka "I'm special," but not always in a good way). This is a quality any* prince can have on the surface, but digging deeper quickly gets past this red herring (*although I've only noticed A-type personalities in Princes 1, 2, 3, and 7). (If you're unsure what is an A-type personality, it's explained at www.JamesSheridan.com/atype.)

The Date

VENUE IDEAS: Let him decide

TARDINESS TOLERANCE: 4 for him, 1 for you.

HIS FAVORITE LETTERS IN WANTED: W and D

Notes: He will usually go on a date with two types of women: potential conquests and potential wife material, although the latter usually catches him by surprise. Putting yourself in the "wife" category is best accomplished by displaying the D as well as the W.

A woman who isn't intimidated by him and won't suffer his "crap" but is respectful. Feeling respected by him is the key to landing your second date.

As If by Magic

Jane's first date was uncannily magical. She was, of course, one jump ahead of her chosen prince, and she hoped for more. Jane will now give the guy a chance to pursue her for a second date, but she's also prepared to ask him if she has to wait too long (taking into account his Tardiness Tolerance). This approach is not to chase; it's because she has a life to live. In any case, she will certainly not stop searching and dating until she and this Prince 5 have agreed to be exclusive.

Does this all sound like "too much work?" Too much like playing games . . . ?

Get real. LIFE is a game.

A "game" is often seen as needlessly playing hard to get, but that's not really a game; that's being a child. If you believe life isn't a game, you believe that we can all go around saying and doing what we want in order to actually get what we want. And you know that isn't true, even in a marriage. (Prince 3 has to learn this the hard way.) Taken in the correct context, a "game" is an appreciation of somebody apart from you who has his own wishes to consider. So, of course, there is a game strategy in dating—as in life!

Dating is a contact sport that's much like sales—networking, calling, following up—but without the chasing. And if it's too much work, you have a choice: you can keep doing the same things and getting the same results, or you can do something different. You only have to find The One, so realize it's a one-time deal—but a deal with a payout that lasts forever.

Two days after her first date, Jane has not yet heard back from Prince 4, but she doesn't run for the Ben and Jerry's. Instead, she browses the dating site for more potential suitors and plans a night out with her friends. Just as she was about to text her girlfriend, she hears a ping on the phone. As if by magic, Prince 4's text says: *"Thanks for coming out, I had a great time! What are you doing Saturday night?"*

Hold the happy dance, WANTED woman, and *focus*.

So, Jane texts back: *"I had a really nice evening, too. Let me check my calendar, and I'll get right back to you."*

Ten minutes later, she puts the guy out of his misery and arranges their second date. (Jane has never had a friend like me.)

part seven

NO
REFUNDS

When Will Your Life Begin Together?

The walk out of your first date to the walk up the aisle is a minefield, but you've possibly laid many of the mines yourself with your preconceived ideas, prejudices, and emotional hang-ups (we all have them). That's not to say that your guy is off the hook, either. You now need to also continually ask yourself, "Is this something that I want?" Let your hair down because this is also his chance to see you for who you truly are and to unconditionally love you.

The final part of our mission involves finding that notorious distinction between fantasy and reality, so you can make an objective assessment. Is this the man you want to spend the rest of your life with? You must see how much of what's going on is truth and how much is in your mind. Confirmation bias becomes an even greater problem as you get more emotionally involved.

Who needs villains when we have ourselves? We are perfectly capable of sabotaging our own happiness without any help. Many of our ancient stories are actually metaphors for the conflict of the light and dark within us. They show us that choosing the light of love, kindness, and compassion is the key to winning the day. But this certain brand of darkness isn't in your genes; you weren't born with it. Rather, *you acquired it* over your lifetime.

Now, you need to apply everything you've read so far in this book to bring it home.

In Part One, you left the wishing well behind, saw through the Two Big Lies (be acutely aware of those now!), and became empowered by the Two Big Revelations.

In Part Two, you applied Big Revelation #2 as you chose your prince from the menu. If you reached the part where you tasted the item you chose and realized it's the wrong choice, you need to take off your blinders. It's possible you chose the wrong prince!

In Part Three, you did the all-important work on yourself to ensure you're forever WANTED. The goal is not to change you but to step into the best version of you. This part of the book becomes especially relevant when facing the minefield you laid down in the real world.

In Part Four, you saw the truth about the Player Problem and how to navigate it, as well as the need to transition from Primal Time to mutual love and intimacy.

Parts Five and Six brought you to this point, as you found your chosen prince and won a date with him. You may find that happened surprisingly fast—much faster than you've been used to if you applied all the techniques correctly.

In Part Seven, you're at the point of making the biggest decision of your life, so do it right. Your next goal is twofold: 1) Make absolutely sure you've chosen correctly and that he is indeed also a good chemistry match and not a player, and 2) If the first goal is met, to keep him forever. When will your life begin together? *Should* it begin? Let's find out.

Movie Night

Let's first take things from your second date to the moment you both agree to be exclusive and enter an intimate relationship. At this intermediary stage, consciously or unconsciously, your prince is facing a spurious dilemma: James Bond lifestyle versus a woman keeping his balls in a Ziploc bag under the sink. Let's help him out of this.

Remember Plato's warning in Part One: "Storytellers are dangerous people." This is because *they have the power to influence behavior at an unconscious level if the message is abstract and subtle.* You underestimate the storyteller's power at your great peril. But you can also use storytellers to your advantage on movie nights.

Certain films are flagged. A few are listed here as I illustrate the challenge you face transitioning from your second date to an exclusive and intimate relationship. You need to swing his decision away from the James Bond lifestyle while showing him you have no intention of keeping his balls in a Ziploc bag under the sink. And why would you want to do that to someone you love, anyway?

Under **"Movies to Never Show Boyfriend,"** you should mentally file the "one vagina for life" film mentioned in Part Four—*Old School.* There is no redemption for the protagonist at the end of this film. Sure, he falls in love with a woman, but in the final scene, she wants to join the frat house (= you should be "cool" like that girl). Banned!

We tend to believe others think exactly as we do, and when it comes to the differences in Primal Time mentality, this doesn't work out. As Dale Carnegie famously pointed out in *How to Win Friends and*

Influence People, he is fond of strawberries, but when he goes fishing, he doesn't use a strawberry as bait; rather, he uses what the fish like. For example, many women are fond of the movies *Dirty Dancing* and *The Notebook*, so it only makes sense to watch those films with the boyfriend, right? Wrong. I'm not exaggerating when I tell you I've often heard a guy say, "Oh, God, she wants me to watch *The Notebook* with her." That's quickly followed by his guy friends consoling him as if his mother just died. This clearly signals that she wants him to be like the men in those films and, heaven forbid, commit to her forever. Too much, too soon.

The moral of those two stories is not subtle. What Plato worried about—and what can work for you *or against you*—is subtlety. *Dirty Dancing* and *The Notebook* should be filed under **"Movies to Never Show Boyfriend."** I know, empathy can be a pain in the ass.

So, what *should* you watch with your boyfriend? In contrast to *Dirty Dancing* and *The Notebook* is the masterpiece *Up in the Air*. This is a classic plot setup of a staunchly single protagonist who, at the *start* of the film, is living a life that CODE RED and YELLOW guys would think is cool. Ryan Bingham (George Clooney) is forever traveling and has a girl in every port. But the Universe steadily sends Bingham more and more signs to wake up. The movie escalates to a pivotal scene in which he has to save his sister's wedding from a groom with cold feet by selling this jittery groom on what this protagonist himself is afraid of: commitment, sacrifice of self to something greater. Eventually, Bingham sees the error of his ways and demonstrates that being a single guy actually sucks.

This movie is a powerful influence on single men because it lures them in by making them identify with the protagonist—and like him. So when the protagonist subtly changes from CODE RED to CODE YELLOW, and then to CODE GREEN, *the male subconscious takes note*, reprogramming his thinking at a deep level. The way Clooney owns the character with such confidence makes the transition all the more meaningful for the male viewer.

Pretty Woman has a similar message to *Up in the Air*, albeit in a fluffier way. But, despite the title of the film and its distinctly feminine poster, it starts off with the surprisingly dark setup of a tycoon playboy who wants a prostitute for a week, just while he's in town. But, like Ryan Bingham, he eventually learns that committing to a woman represents a better life than the shallow one he was leading before. He even demonstrates this in a tongue-in-cheek way at the end of the film, which appeals to the man who thinks the fairy tale is "sissy stuff."

From a man's perspective, it's a shame about the title *Pretty Woman*. (Titles matter. For example, I like the taste of "Skinny Girl" margarita mix, but when the guy at the checkout gives me a funny look, I have to say, "It's for my sister" with a nervous laugh. Welcome to Guy World.) I would retitle this movie to make it more appealing to average male viewers still possibly on Primal Time. *Up in the Air* and ~~*Pretty Woman*~~ *The Playboy Who Hired a Hooker for a Whole Week* should be filed under **"Movies to Brainwash Boyfriend With."**

Why do men sleep with you and then fall off the face of the planet? Because they're scared to tell you they simply don't want to see you anymore. Why? Because they're terrified you'll go psycho on them. It's like that scene from *Fatal Attraction* when Michael Douglas's character, after having a brief extramarital affair with Glenn Close's character, tries to break it off with her. Just when he thinks she's agreeing and invites him over for a farewell hug, he sees blood and realizes she's slashed her wrists. You have no idea how much that one scene makes the blood drain from men's faces —and how it traumatized a generation of single men. If he tells you he doesn't want to see you anymore or simply disappears, he might be unconsciously worried that you'll slash your wrists and bleed over his new Armani suit—or, even worse, scratch his car. *Fatal Attraction* should be urgently filed under **"Movies to Never, EVER Show Boyfriend."** Once you're married and fidelity is the greater concern, then you should file *Fatal Attraction* under **"Movies to Brainwash Husband With,"** but that's a different book.

Command that TV remote, girl, and if it gets into his hands and you see him about to click on a flagged movie, dive in front of the TV as if taking a bullet for the president. Then land on his lap in a sexy pose and say, "Let's go to bed!"

James Bond vs. Ziploc bag. Get it? Okay, let's fire some bullets at this next challenge:

Second Date and Beyond

- That first kiss can tell you a great deal, especially to literally confirm chemistry. But then there's dealing with that awkward moment on the doorstep when you both know the first kiss is due. Know your prince's profile (more in the breakout session). How do you know if he wants to kiss or not? As long as he didn't part your company like a FedEx man delivering a package, he *does* want to kiss you, but he usually needs a little encouragement (dependent on Genetype). As usual, seek a balance. Don't pounce on him so fast that he reaches for the rape whistle (and remember to feed The Virgin Delusion). And don't stand there with eyes closed and lips pouted looking like a sleeping duck. Simply lock eyes and tell him what a kissable mouth he has. Then let him lead. If he doesn't, tell him how much you'd like to kiss his mouth. If he doesn't kiss you then, well, he's either intoxicated or gay.

- Keep the Playdar on but without getting overly suspicious or possessive, or he will run. Be objective, deal with facts, and remember male differences from Part Four.

- Texting is only telling you so much, so go to video or phone calls but in measured ways.

- How hard is he working to secure your affections? Keep the answer to this question squarely in the context of which prince he is! If he hasn't called you for a while, don't cut off your hair. Instead, consider which type he is, and then ask him why he hasn't called. Be direct, be Assertive.

- At this stage, booty calls are inappropriate. Don't brush him off completely; he's just on Primal Time. Simply postpone to a regular time. Be Tasteful and Dignified. Don't forget what you learned in our classroom when you get into the real world and stay WANTED!

The Sexual Part

- Most men suddenly grow a brain when it comes to getting sex, and they know "The Three-Date Rule." Yes, a player will simply wait for the third date. Trust your gut! For you, there is no such rule or expectation; sex happens when you feel comfortable and not a moment sooner. This moment is typically when you feel you're both connected, when hooked on each other, when you sense he'd rather be with you than somewhere else. He cherishes your body, but he doesn't mindlessly grope at it. This is the difference between having sex (a Primal Time animal) and making love (a compassionate human being).

- Don't be self-conscious about any physical flaws. What you hate about yourself he may not have a problem with, so do not say anything negative about yourself unless you're making a joke out of it. Don't plant ideas, or he might think, "Oh, I never noticed, but now that she mentions it . . ."

- Feed The Virgin Delusion! (as already discussed several times). The balance is between being good in bed but not too good. A good trick is to ask him advice on sexual tips and techniques (= I'm not that experienced). As you perform sexual acts on him, ask, "Do you like that?" This puts you in the experimentation category as opposed to the pro category. Be sure you're in a position to tell him you've "never done that before" about a particular act. You never want to come across too much like you know what you're doing. And you want him to believe that no other man can make you feel the way he does.

• This book doesn't focus on sexual technique, but let me offer a few tips. Many women have questions about performing fellatio well. My short and simple answer? Imagine you're eating an ice cream. The more his penis needs hardening, the gentler you need to be. Do not force it or create any pressure or show any disappointment; if it's not happening, move to something else such as kissing or stroking.

• After a first sexual encounter, the most common complaint is about penis size/shape/length/hardness/technique, etc. Get off Primal Time. The female orgasm is induced at two points that have little to do with penis length or other physical characteristics. Because the pressure is all on the man to perform, he's likely nervous and/or still building feelings for you that lead to better erections as the relationship unfolds. It takes a while to "find your groove," so give it time and keep at it. Men need to feel adequate, so be sure you tell him how good it was, even if you don't mean it at this stage. If you don't say so, then you increase the risk of him not calling you again, and then you'll call him a player!

• If you need to fake an orgasm, do it right. If you don't arch your back forward and curl your toes down as you shudder, an experienced man will be onto you. And on that first sexual encounter, you may well need to. Remember, you want him to feel *adequate.*

• For middle-aged men and upward, it's perfectly possible and natural that he has some degree of erectile dysfunction. Viagra has fixed that and then some, and he knows it. Response times for Viagra are one to two hours, so no surprise sex for that age group (unless you want him to feel inadequate). If you tell him you'll be over in ten minutes and that he'd better be waiting in bed, he might find a reason not to be available for an hour or two. It's not that he doesn't want you; chances are he's on Viagra. Accept that this is a medical reality for most men at some point. It strikes at the heart of feeling adequate, so be gentle around this topic.

The Deeper Assessment

- If you're confused about any actions or reactions of his, reference his prince profile to keep it in context. If you're still puzzled, consider that you may have assessed his type incorrectly.

- This book is called *Kiss Fewer Frogs*, not *Kiss Zero Frogs*. It's possible you got the wrong prince profile, and there's no shame in that. Just because you're already "invested" in the relationship, it's smart still to cut your losses, wash him out of your hair, and decisively move on. It's a simple numbers game until you find The One, so don't settle for the wrong choice out of convenience.

- Does he take you out and/or show you off to friends and family?

- Tell him when it's your period. Does he still want to be with you even when sex isn't desirable for you?

- Being brutally honest, is he truly your chosen prince type? And if he is, is there truly chemistry there? Did you choose the correct prince type in the first place? Keep an open mind; don't let confirmation bias sway you!

If all is going well, we can move on to the next stage of the relationship. Ask yourself this important question:

Is It Love?

Too often, we confuse a cheap imitation of love with the real thing, thinking we've found love when we haven't. In fact, you might be just playing the starring role in your own romantic comedy. The "confirmation bias" mentioned earlier refers to only seeing what you want to see instead of truth—and bias can also apply to love. Many people never find someone they *truly* love, but they may never have experienced the real thing either, so are none the wiser. So, your next task must be to ensure you are *truly* getting this need met, and that requires a better understanding of love and its imitators.

Infatuation

This is defined as "an intense but short-lived crush," but it's more love-based than lust, which is something of a relationship albeit possibly one way. In your search for the real thing, infatuation is a potential trap to fall into. People are often quick to dismiss infatuation, but I see it as love's skirmishers as you scout for potential love and compatibility. Unlike *lust* that appeals to the physical, *infatuation* can appeal to the metaphysical—that is, he can get inside your head, just not your underwear. Notice it says "head," not "heart." If you're unsure, as with lust, all you can do is wait it out, perhaps explore it, and see what it turns into, if anything.

Infatuation can be a one-way street, though, so tread carefully. You don't want to unilaterally develop deep feelings and fall into the bitter scenario of unrequited love—or become a notch on someone's bedpost.

In Love

Being *in* love is almost its own thing—like a force in play that's out of your control or comprehension. An incurable virus takes hold, and the chemistry between you exists beyond reason. It can be instant chemistry, or it can grow. It's a spell that can last a long time or pass quickly into the night. It can be the prelude to something greater or simply fade away. Relationships may have waves of this force at different times. Falling in love may birth a relationship; falling out of love may kill a relationship. *It depends on the type of love that underpins it.*

Perhaps the clue to understanding this state is the verb that *in love* is married to: *falling.* This indicates having no control over it, a common hazard regularly spending time with someone, and you say, "It just happened." When you "fall," you could land on your feet, you could not fall far, or you could splatter all over.

Conditional Love

Typically in the realm of established relationships, if your love for a person diminishes when he hurts you, it's *conditional* love (although not to discount it as love). Even if someone does take a place in your heart, you need to know exactly what you're both feeling. Is what you are giving and receiving *true* love?

Conditional love is still love and will therefore satisfy your need for love, but the hazard is inherent in the name. Imagine a relationship as a reservoir. Over time, a couple fills that reservoir with their love for each other. As long as they continually replenish it, there is no reason why conditional love won't satisfy.

But, in the travails of real life, hurt is inevitable, and each time one person hurts the other, the reservoir level drops. Worse still and more common is that, with continual hurt, the reservoir and the relationship get frozen over with no way of replenishing them. The couple slips under the ice unfulfilled, their need for love is not met. They may retain a sense of belonging from the companionship and settle for living in a comfort zone. But as life unfolds, especially when children leave the nest, the ice that remains simply shatters. Something within yearns for life's greater experience.

I fear *conditional* love is what most relationships are based on. It's the result of charging into a relationship without being whole, without loving oneself first. Most of us are incomplete in a dysfunctional way, and we often see a partner as a way of completing ourselves, yet only one person can truly complete you—and that's you. I appreciate you can't just easily walk away, and walls are hard to tear down, but there is no reason why conditional love can't transform into something better *if both people are on board*.

Unconditional (True) Love

This kind of relationship is like a growing tree, not a reservoir. Any hurt comes like a storm that sways the branches but not the trunk of this tree. What is that trunk? True, unconditional love, deeply rooted into your heart and soul. Even if this tree were violently cut down, the roots remain forever. True love can make you whole, but you have a greater opportunity to find true love if you are whole first.

The closer I am to explaining true love, the harder it gets, and the more I realize you have to *feel it* to know it. You can love a person so much that you'd let him go if it meant he would be happier without you, even though it could destroy you. A wall of selfishness is breached by involuntary sacrifice, and true love is perfect kindness born of the heart. *You must seek someone who loves you for who you really are.* It's such a cliché but so true. Without experiencing love, a person would see it as an empty cliché. You don't have to "work" at a kind of relationship that's filled with unconditional love (although you shouldn't take that fact for granted). Its end can be a beautiful death, an honored and effortless *sacrifice*.

Soul Reunion Love

"O happy dagger! This is thy sheath. There rust, and let me die," says Juliet, right before she kills herself over Romeo's death. The deeper you go, the closer you get to what is not *meant* to be understood; you just have to experience the mystical sublime. Any clumsy attempt to explain this is perhaps best said in these three words:

♛

You just know.

Something in the meeting of the eyes goes deeper than any type of love previously discussed, yet it features *all* those types of love.

Two people meet as if they're magnets helplessly drawn together by a smell, a sense. *They somehow know each other yet they are strangers.* "Union of souls" doesn't cut it; this is somehow a "*re*union."

"Soul Mate" is often an overworked, incorrectly used phrase that wishful-thinking couples banter around simply because they're together or feel one of the previously described states. As a Soul Mate, you are permanently and constantly *in* love; *true* love is an understatement; *lust* is a gateway to a condition of what can only be described as a transcendent state of *dissolution* into one another —a state that's outside space, time, and one another.

Mother Nature can play cruel tricks on you, so don't let wishful thinking (confirmation bias) convince you of something in play that this is not. Time will show you if a Soul Mate is what you have attracted. More than a tree, think of it as an ancient enchanted forest, and these twinned souls are involuntarily blended into it.

To say more about this seems sacrilegious; I simply can't do justice to its description. You will only know this if you meet your Soul Mate, *and that means getting out of your own way so opportunity may present itself.* I have no way of knowing if there are multiple Soul Mates for you or just one, but if you're not connected to The Energy Field—if you're not present and open to the moment—then the question becomes irrelevant.

If what you have is true love, what's next? Let's transition into managing this relationship in daily life.

Are You Speaking His Language?

As you merge the dating world with the relationship world, let me hand the microphone to Gary Chapman and his excellent book, *The Five Love Languages*. Chapman explains that we each give and receive love in ONE of five ways: Physical Touch, Quality Time, Words of Affirmation, Gifts, and Acts of Service. If two people in a relationship speak different love languages, each might feel like he or she is giving love but the other person still doesn't feel loved.

Chapman admits there's a complication with the love languages— that each of these love languages mean different things to different people. Yet it's a complication that awareness of Genetypes fixes. For example, let's say two different men both have the same love language of Gifts. What one man sees as a gift, the other man may not. Let's say one man is a Prince 5 and the other a Prince 7. If you gave a gift of a designer watch to a Prince 5, for example, he'd probably want to take it back to the store and have the money instead, but a Prince 7 would love it. In this way, you can customize any of these love languages according to Genetype.

Find out the love language of your man as quickly as possible, and speak that language to him so he feels loved. You can usually tell his love language preference because it's what he complains most about not getting! Also, be sure to explain to him *your* love language and say what *you* need to feel loved. (In the breakout session, you'll find each love language customized for each prince.)

If both parties in a relationship feel loved,
then all is well. Awareness of love languages,
WHEN customized by Genetype, is the key.

But is there only ONE love language per person? Yes, but many people who've read the book believe they have TWO love languages, referred to as a primary and secondary love language. I believe that Genetypes are causing this confusion, explained through my own example:

I'm a Prince 3, and, like all arty Prince 3s, I need Words of Affirmation. This is because, like any creative person (writer/chef/musician/painter, etc.), we want our creation to be enjoyed. That means I feel loved when people give me good feedback—but not in the romantic sense. So, here's where the confusion exists.

In a relationship, I need to give and receive love by Physical Touch. So, the likely secondary Love Language of a Prince 3—the Genetypal Love Language—is Words of Affirmation. But his true love language —what he needs to actually feel romantically loved and how he expresses romantic love—appears to be random.

So, don't be confused about what is the true love language of you or another person. If two love languages exist, bear in mind that one likely relates to the Dominant Driver of that Genetype. (You'll find the likely Genetypal Love Language of each prince in the breakout session that follows.)

The Five Love Languages is an incredibly powerful tool in relationships. However, it could be completely blunted if it's not sharpened by your awareness of Genetypes specific to your prince's profile.

Breakout Session: Playing for Keeps

Notes on this breakout session:

- Passion Level is given on a scale of 1 to 5, with 5 being the highest. This lets you know if the level of passion he shows you is merely a function of his profile. For example, if his profile indicates he's a passionate person but he's not being passionate with you, you know there's a problem. Conversely, if his profile shows him as not a particularly passionate person, then you know it's his nature not to be.

- Examples of customizing each of the Five Love Languages is shown, as well as a *speculation* about his secondary Genetypal Love Language. Physical Touch is omitted because it is universal by type. Once you know your prince's specific Love Language, you can customize it accordingly.

- Fear of Commitment level is given on a scale of 1 to 5, with 5 being the highest level of fear. This allows you to take into account how much of any fear of commitment is a function of his nature versus your relationship with him.

- I Love You Factor is rated 1 to 5, with 5 being most inclined to tell you he loves you and express his feelings to you. This is particularly useful early in a relationship when you're gauging if he loves you or not—as well as how likely he will say "I love you" before you do.

- You'll also get a deeper understanding of each prince's dark side as well as how to manage it. That can indicate if the issue is due to his nature and not you.

• Best of all, you'll see how to use Big Revelation #2: how to empower him and be the woman who makes him become all he can be. This stems from his Dominant Driver. Some princes will already be living their purpose in life (usually when it aligns with what society wants men to do/be). Others, though, might need the empowerment you can give.

Keeping Prince 1:

Passion level: 1

Fear of commitment level: 1

Love Language customization:
- Quality Time ideas: Events to do with his work
- Words of Affirmation ideas: Praise his career successes
- Gift ideas: Designer pen, engraved business card holder, anything to use in work or hang in his office
- Acts of Service ideas: Sacrifice for his career, letting him work late without complaining, supporting his goals
- *Possible* secondary (Genetypal) Love Language: Acts of Service

"I Love You" Factor: 1

How to help him deal with his dark side:

Life is not the black-and-white world he wants it to be, so help him deal with this reality and understand that not all problems are meant to be solved. Encourage spontaneity so he can see the rewards of it and where it takes him. He needs to develop an "off" switch to separate his professional from his personal life.

How to empower him:

This is one of the easiest princes to empower, because he's likely already doing what he's meant to do: pursuing a successful career in the corporate world. If he's not already doing this, then this is a great opportunity for you to help him find his true self. Otherwise, there are two ways you can empower him further: 1) Give unwavering support for his career, understanding it's his joy. 2) Be sure he isn't tempted to be an entrepreneur. He needs leaders to serve under and receive counsel from. He can struggle for direction without it.

Keeping Prince 2:

Passion level: 3

Fear of commitment level: 4

Love Language customization:

- Quality Time ideas: Studying/learning/traveling together
- Words of Affirmation ideas: Praising his intellect and ability to relay it
- Gift ideas: Whatever hobby or interest he's currently deep into
- Acts of Service ideas: Deep and meaningful conversations, a sounding board for his ideas, space and alone time
- *Possible* secondary (Genetypal) Love Language: Acts of Service

"I Love You" Factor: 2

How to help him deal with his dark side:

He needs to learn to connect with people, muster more acceptance of the human condition, feel triumphant, and have one great love in his life: you. Help him accept the world for the crazy mess that it is. Awaken that spiritual part, which can help him with that acceptance.

How to empower him:

You have a great opportunity here. This is a man who can influence others and garner a great following, but he needs to embrace the world and ways to accomplish that, instead of retreating from it. Become a part of his richer, inner world; join him on what could be a fascinating journey.

Keeping Prince 3:

Passion level: 5

Fear of commitment level: 3

Love Language customization:

- Quality Time ideas: Sharing in or participating in his creative interests and art, brainstorming together, deep romance

- Words of Affirmation ideas: Praise his creations

- Gift ideas: Instrument of choice (pen/guitar/paint, etc.)

- Acts of Service ideas: Promoting his creation, giving him space to create, a sounding board

- *Possible* secondary (Genetypal) Love Language: Words of Affirmation

"I Love You" Factor: 5

How to help him deal with his dark side:

This guy is like a sports car—exciting but runs hot. Whenever fury is triggered in him, he struggles to control it, even if he knows it's not doing him any favors. At those times, adding fuel to the fire is the worst thing you can do. Just let the fire burn out, and when it does, he'll be back to normal, wondering what just happened. The great opportunity here for a partner is to not take his meltdowns personally. Rather, you want to help him get between his emotions and his actions, and to encourage him to react to facts instead of what he perceives as facts. This would be a rare and prized find for him.

How to empower him:

Two huge opportunities exist: 1) To help him become the creative artist he's meant to be but doesn't know it. 2) To become The Muse to an existing creative artist. Reflect closely on his childhood together. What did he love doing and was good at? His creative nature may have been long buried by ego and societal pressure.

Keeping Prince 4:

Passion level: 4

Fear of commitment level: 4

Love Language customization:

- Quality Time ideas: Dining, partying, sexual exploration

- Words of Affirmation ideas: He's amazing as he is. It doesn't matter to him what society says a man should be/do; money isn't what it's about.

- Gift ideas: Books about philosophy

- Acts of Service ideas: Sexual acts, allowing him to go out by himself, anything that lets him escape the idle conformity of society

- *Possible* secondary (Genetypal) Love Language: Physical Touch

"I Love You" Factor: 5

How to help him deal with his dark side:

Help him experience the rewards of romantic commitment to just one person for life and explore a metaphysical place you've both yet to touch. His obsession with women is an unconscious quest to find something that doesn't exist: the perfect woman. If you can *subtly* help him come to terms with that, you would win a great partner.

How to empower him:

His true purpose in life is often unknown to him, and it's related to his obsession with women: philosophy, the study of the nature of existence. (Because women create life through birth, this is goddess worship.) It's a great opportunity for the woman who can lead him to his true but deeply hidden purpose. Dare I say, he might see you as that "perfect" woman at the end of his quest.

Keeping Prince 5:

Passion level: 4

Fear of commitment level: 5

Love Language customization:

- Quality Time ideas: Camping, boating, hiking, enjoying nature and outdoors

- Words of Affirmation ideas: Praise his ultimate goal of doing whatever he wants each day

- Gift ideas: Outdoors/camping/boating accessories, etc., something related to whatever it is he does most when he's enjoying alone time

- Acts of Service ideas: Grant him alone time, make allowances for lack of timekeeping

- *Possible* secondary (Genetypal) Love Language: Acts of Service

"I Love You" Factor: 4

How to help him deal with his dark side:

Show him that freedom and commitment to a life partner don't have to be mutually exclusive. If children are in your life or could be in your future, let his natural connection with them underpin your relationship. The Ziploc bag fear is your biggest enemy with this guy, so negate that fear as your highest priority without sacrificing your own needs.

How to empower him:

Chances are he's already fully engaged in living a life centered around his true purpose of freedom, but if he isn't—his spirit having been crushed by a cubicle somewhere—then your opportunity is huge. Maybe there's a way for him to integrate his need for freedom with making a living. Most of all, show him that freedom is what it's all about, and that society has it all wrong.

Keeping Prince 6:

Passion level: 4

Fear of commitment level: 3

Love Language customization:

- Quality Time ideas: He can enjoy most things together as long as not too "girly"

- Words of Affirmation ideas: Praise his manliness

- Gift ideas: Man cave accessories, sports tickets, security-related items

- Acts of Service ideas: Allow guys' nights without keeping time

- *Possible* secondary (Genetypal) Love Language: Acts of Service

"I Love You" Factor: 2

How to help him deal with his dark side:

Help him see the value of diplomacy. His tendency to constantly feel threatened and react physically could be a problem domestically, so let him see the value in not quickly flying off the handle or getting physical. He's thinks in literal, black-and-white ways, so he will respond to a cause-and-effect "rules" system. Help him become a "spiritual warrior" on the path of self-control.

How to empower him:

Your greatest opportunity occurs if you see his soul fading because he's at a desk job or similar. This man needs to be where the action is (see Part Five for likely vocations), so showing him his true purpose could be of massive value. If he's already living his true purpose, get behind that, support him, and appreciate the service he's giving to the world.

Keeping Prince 7:

Passion level: 3

Fear of commitment level: 2

Love Language customization:

- Quality Time ideas: Enjoying the spoils of success together

- Words of Affirmation ideas: Respect, respect, respect

- Gift ideas: Symbols of power that he can show to others

- Acts of Service ideas: Anything to demonstrate loyalty and unwavering support, especially in the darkest hours (which are likely to occur on occasion)

- *Possible* secondary (Genetypal) Love Language: Words of Affirmation

"I Love You" Factor: 2

How to help him deal with his dark side:

For self-confident people, the only thing that can lose respect from others is when their confidence falls over the knife-edge that divides it from arrogance. You must diplomatically help him keep that balance. Don't let him walk all over you by demonstrating strict, severe consequences for doing so. Deep down, he *wants* to show his emotions to those he loves, but he struggles to do so. If you become his "emotional microphone," your effort will go a long way.

How to empower him:

He's likely already engaged in his life purpose through some kind of leadership, but you can help him become a better leader. A good leader sees how ruling by compassion, not self-service, is true power and gets better results. The challenge is letting him see that being emotional in the form of compassion is not a weakness; it is a strength. Greater rewards come automatically when one does the right thing by others.

• • •

See the Light

Time and love are your most precious commodities, but I argue that love is the more valuable of the two. Our life spans may be measured by the sands of time, but would we even care how fast the sand slipped through our fingers if it measured a life without love? Your life is incomplete without love, and you only have so much time to find it. Just as many people say, "Time is money," I want you to start saying, "Time is love." I trust this book has granted you these precious commodities and lifted the fog on Planet Dating.

Your fairy tale ending is waiting for you to take it. It may not look exactly as you always imagined, but it's *real*. Whatever you choose on the Seven Princes menu, make sure you choose wisely so you can put the "ever after" into "happily." There are no refunds in this restaurant. If you choose a cheeseburger, don't later complain about heartburn. If you choose a salad, don't later complain about not having your hunger satisfied.

Life is a continually bittersweet trade-off, but it's a life worth sharing with the right person. You are an equal team, walking up the mountain together, each member with strengths and weaknesses. When one person falls, the other picks him or her up with unconditional love and sacrifice. Oneness is won—a grand prize worth winning.

Now, go plant your flag at the summit.

• • •

Back to my daughter's story time. My mental rewrite of the tale concluded as I turned the final page and glanced at her. Little Scarlett had fallen asleep. I gazed upon her innocent face, glowing against the nightlight. *"Once upon a time there was a princess."* And what adventures she will have!

I gently unclipped her cone-shaped princess hat, tucked her in, and kissed a chubby cheek. Then I whispered the final line of the book to her:

"And they lived happily ever after."

Afterword:

Mirror, Mirror

Part Three explained that you can't love someone properly until you first love yourself. But how can you love yourself if you don't know who you truly are? How would you know who it is you're loving? *The You Code* will tell you.

As a thank you for buying *Kiss Fewer Frogs,* download the first chapter of *The You Code* for free at www.JamesSheridan.com/kfftyc1. Enjoy!

Acknowledgments

My publisher, Gail Woodard, thanks for being more than a publisher; you're also a mentor and practically my manager. The Dudley Court Press team (Carrie, Lora, Winsome, Chris and Morgan). My editors, Barbara McNichol and Pam Nordberg, thanks for getting me and making me a better writer than I otherwise would be. Kathi Dunn, Tina Nguyen, Vanessa Stokes, Linda Barbara, Laterria K. Jones, Heather Leet, and Bernice Grullion—thanks for all your great contributions and feedback. Linda Sheridan and Jen Sheridan, I don't deserve your amazing support and kindness. As a special thanks to you, my reader, for being one of the few to actually read these acknowledgments, a free consultation is waiting for you by registering at JamesSheridan.com/wow. Thanks to all the supportive *You Code* readers, fans, and followers, especially those in the focus group and beta testers for *Kiss Fewer Frogs*. And thanks to all my clients and seminar attendees. Our ongoing work as a team helped shape this work.

More By James Sheridan

The YOU Code

**Don't *'change'* who you are.
'Awaken' to it.**

No matter what you've been through in life, there is a force inside you that has not and cannot be taken away from you because it is you. Its spirit is irrepressible and inde-structible, and **this** is your search and rescue mission for it.

International bestselling author James Sheridan uncovers the missing connections between ancient history, genetics, and a for-gotten but powerful psychological theory. *The YOU Code* defies the conventional self-improvement message of changing who you are, and instead invites you to awaken to your true self. This groundbreaking self-improvement system also succinctly shows you:

- How your purpose in life is derived from your ancient and hidden lineage, peace and clarity from a life built on your predestined definition of "success"

- Why every relationship has genetic flashpoints, and how to master them

- The three ancient truths that cut through all the health and diet confusion

- The two sacred cycles that grant you mastery of money

This provocative page-turner provides definitive answers to the most important questions you'll ever ask yourself: "Who am I and why am I here?" It's time to discover what you once were and what's still living inside you, awaiting rebirth.

More by James Sheridan

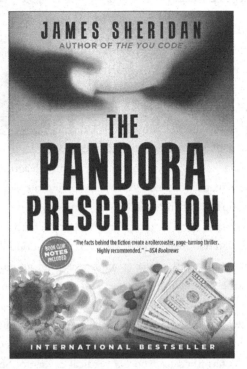

Author Dan Travis, a specialist on notorious unsolved mysteries, is on a book tour when a cryptic message plunges him into a silent war hinging on an incriminating data file. Finding it is Travis' only hope for surviving a deadly cross country chase. But to do so, he must discover the link between an extraordinary cover-up by Big Pharma and the assassination of JFK. The key lies within a secret underground of doctors sworn to an ancient oath. James Sheridan's crackling prose and driving narrative make this novel a white-knuckle ride through America's hidden corridors of power.

James Sheridan

James Sheridan is an award-winning, international best-selling author, speaker, business consultant, award-winning copywriter, and founder of an Inc. 5000 corporation. Originally from London, England, Sheridan started from humble beginnings before embarking on an eclectic journey of diverse careers and accomplishments. He has been a professional ice hockey player in Britain's premier league, the youngest regional sales manager for FIAT Auto Group, and a commercial airline pilot. His first pilot job included flying cargo to the Caribbean and secretive diplomatic mail flights from Miami to Cuba in unmarked aircraft as a foreign national. Later he flew 737s from London Heathrow.

Sheridan resigned his career as an airline pilot at age twenty-nine to start businesses, invest in real estate, and trade financial markets. He was determined to unlock the shortcuts and secrets of all aspects of life. He then passed on these shortcuts and secrets to tens of thousands of students around the globe through his highly successful company.

In 2007, determined to expose a medical cover-up, Sheridan wrote the fact-based novel *The Pandora Prescription,* which became a best seller in America and China. Sheridan has dedicated the last twenty years to finding the definitive answers for humanity's biggest questions, and his groundbreaking book *The You Code* represented the conclusion of his quest. Building on his Genetypal theory explained in *The You Code,* James Sheridan presents the ultimate dating solution: *Kiss Fewer Frogs.*

Connect with James online at:

 JamesSheridan.com

www.facebook.com/groups/kissfewerfrogs